Writing from within
Workbook

Praise for Bernard Selling's work

"ABC Learn has had a great deal of success in teaching literacy to at-risk youths and others who have minimal English skills. Probably 50 percent of the success we have had in the past few years can be attributed to Bernard Selling's writing method. His *Life Story Writing (Story Telling) Workbook I* and the workshops he has given our teachers embrace the best method for teaching writing that I have encountered. This workbook provides our tutors and students with a great number of writing skills, while encouraging students to express deeply imbedded feelings about their life experiences."

— Debra Greenfield, CEO of ABC Learn (see Oprah Winfrey's website for *Precious* for more about ABC Learn)

"Bernard Selling's impressive new *Life Story Writing: Self-Awareness/Relationship Workbook III* guides us on our way to an examined life. It enhances our understanding of how we are with those we love and don't love along this path and assists us to know ourselves better while developing skills to express that knowledge in written words as we search our deep well of experience for clues to who we are. Addressing many levels of self-discovery and creative thinking and written in a clear and interesting style, the workbook will be extremely useful with secondary and college students. Adults will love it, too. I especially found the thought-provoking questions invaluable. We are all engaged in the endless search for identity. Who am I, where am I going, and with whom… it never stops. Can one ever know too much about oneself?"

— Paula Diggs, MA English, MA School Counseling, MS Family Therapy. California State University Northridge, Department of Education (retired), Special Education Counselor (retired)

DEDICATION

To Isabel and Max

Also by Bernard Selling

Writing from Within
Writing from Within: The Next Generation
Writing from Deeper Within
The Art of Seeing
Character Consciousness
The Duke's Musician (novel)
Predators (novel)
The da Vinci Intrusion (novel)
Fortune's Smile (novel)
Henry, Boy of Barrio (film)
First Year, A.D. (film)
Three Miraculous Soldiers (film)
The Flying Machine (film)

Writing from within
Workbook

Bernard Selling

— • • • —

I had reached the age of thirty-eight
and wanted to assess my life—
figure out what had gone wrong,
what had gone right.

I started at the beginning;
I started with my first memory.
As soon as I remembered the first memory of my life,
everything started to flow.

❧

STING, 1991

Hunter House
PUBLISHERS

Copyright © 2013 by Bernard Selling

Hunter House Inc., Publishers
An imprint of Turner Publishing Company
www.turnerpublishing.com

Library of Congress Cataloging-in-Publication Data
Selling, Bernard.
Writing from within workbook / Bernard Selling.
    pages   cm
ISBN 978-0-89793-630-9 (pbk) — ISBN 978-0-89793-684-2 (ebook)
    ISBN 978-0-89793-686-6 (spiral bound)
1. Autobiography—Authorship—Problems, exercises, etc. 2. Creative writing—
Problems, exercises, etc. 3. Authorship—Problems, exercises, etc. I. Title.
CT25.S455 2012
808.06'692—dc23   2012030031

Project Credits
Cover Design: Brian Dittmar Design, Inc.
Book Production: John McKercher
Developmental Editors: Amy Bauman and Jack Duffy
Copy Editor: Susan Lyn McCombs
Proofreader: Martha Scarpati
Managing Editor: Alexandra Mummery
Editorial Intern: Tu-Anh Dang-Tran
Acquisitions Coordinator: Susan Lyn McCombs
Special Sales Manager: Judy Hardin
Publicity Coordinator: Martha Scarpati
Rights Coordinator: Candace Groskreutz
Customer Service Manager: Christina Sverdrup
Order Fulfillment: Washul Lakdhon
Administrator: Theresa Nelson
Computer Support: Peter Eichelberger
Publisher: Kiran S. Rana

Manufactured in the United States of America

9 8 7 6 5 4 3 2   First Edition   13 14 15 16 17

Contents

Unit II: Advanced Steps in Writing Life Stories and Fiction 39

Preface

The "writing from within" method was created for you to have at your fingertips a very different, effective way of learning and developing writing skills—one that is easy to grasp, helpful in overcoming fears of writing, and useful in assisting everyone interested in writing about himself or herself, regardless of age, background, and ethnicity, to become aware of and channel feelings into a safe, appropriate place.

This volume is intended both as a companion to *Writing from Deeper Within* and *Writing from Within: The Next Generation.* It can also be used independently of the other books. The purpose of this workbook is to help you get the feel of writing about different kinds of moments in your life and to see that command of even the simplest of sentences gives you great power of self-expression. The workbook prepares you to explore, and express in a vivid way, personal moments in your life and then to launch yourself into other kinds of creative writing: novels, short stories, and screenplays as well as creative nonfiction.

From time to time in this workbook, I refer to writing techniques that appear later in the book. When I make such references, my intention is not to digress but to give you, the reader, a sense that many of the techniques discussed in this book are deeply intertwined. Likewise, I often mention films and musical and theatrical pieces. On first glance these discussions or mentions may seem to be digressions, but they are not. No matter the medium of expression, the production of creative work is always somewhat similar. As a lifelong musician, photographer, play and film director, screenwriter, and novelist, I have come to see the remarkable similarities that exist so strongly in the many art forms that I have explored. The selections I have made, to illustrate various points along the way, come from stories that may be found in the "Stories" section of this workbook.

Assumptions Revisited

As I sat down to write this exercise book, I began to reflect on the things I had learned about teaching writing over the past thirty years. Looking back, it became evident to me that I, and many of my colleagues, had made three assumptions about writing that were questionable at best.

First, we had driven into our students' heads the notion that, for them to write well, they must first learn all about sentence structure, grammar, usage, and the like.

Second, we had taught them that, in order to write well, they had to know how to read on a high level.

Third, we had taught them that their voices in the world were not important. "Learn to think and write objectively," most of us had been taught, and so we demanded the same of our students, even at a very young age.

My experience has shown me that none of these assumptions are correct. I have found that by using the simple language learned in personal writing, writers are able to find their own authentic writing voices quickly and easily, with their fears under control. They are able to write and rewrite with confidence and an understanding of the rewards that rewriting brings. It is trying to learn complicated language structures before one learns the power of simple structure that defeats a budding writer.

In fact, far from needing to know the complexities of grammar, a command of simple subject-verb-object sentences is the only requirement for doing personal writing. Once that is understood, the student is diverted from grammar and usage toward feelings, dialogue, and innermost thoughts, giving him the chance to see how much he can accomplish with his natural voice. Likewise, the assumption that the higher the reading level, the better the writing is also questionable. My experience is that extensive and sophisticated reading leads, more often than not, to inflated and pretentious writing unless a writer has first done a considerable amount of personal writing. In fact, in my experience, the more a writer explores personal writing, the more he opens himself to understanding and enjoying the writing of others.

The third assumption that I question is our devotion to teaching writers to write objectively without first teaching them ways to value themselves and their feelings in the world. That means they must understand and experience their feelings in safe ways, a safety that seldom takes place when they deal with objective writing (in as much as objective writing is almost always about what is or isn't true and is therefore a judgment with which the reader may argue). It also means that we as teachers/workshop leaders must find ways to give them feedback about their work that is positive, nonjudgmental, and supportive.

True, my observations may be colored by my own life experience: The reading I did when I was younger convinced me that I would never be able to write as well as the writers whom I had read. Moreover, whatever facility I had with words led me toward inflated, impersonal, pretentious language. This kept me at arm's length from my readers. It took me many years to overcome this problem.

Overcoming the Fear of Writing

For many of us, putting our thoughts and feelings down on paper causes great anxiety. Whether we are teachers or students, writing professionals or people from other lands hoping for a better life, the fear is there.

It took me many decades to understand and harness my own fears of writing. As the son of a highly educated, psychiatrist/author father, I was accustomed to thinking independently from an early age. Writing lengthy term papers, even in junior high school, was not daunting. But I shied away from other kinds of writing, either personal or creative. Although I read widely, I couldn't imagine actually writing about myself or about fictional characters. "Nobody wants to hear about you and your opinions," my teachers would say in school. "Don't get self-absorbed." I got the message: "You are not important." Likewise, my father, a man of science, was objective about almost everything. I assumed they were right: I was not important, and the only valuable writing was impersonal writing.

Then, when I was sixteen, my father died. I found myself wanting to hide from everyone and everything. I turned away from all the things I enjoyed doing—music, athletics, dating. I had no one to turn to and no means for expressing my aloneness.

As I began my career as a college writing teacher, in my early twenties, I tried writing creatively again. However, always ready to criticize myself, I would begin correcting whatever I had written a page or two into any story. Then the story idea would slip away and I would give up. This went on for several years. Finally I gave up trying to write in a creative way.

After a few years of college teaching, I went into the film industry, directing documentaries and later short fiction films. I began studying the art of directing actors under the guidance of Lee Strasberg of the Actors Studio. What a joy that was! In working with the actors' imaginations, I could create endlessly. My "self-critic" slept, and my innermost "creative self" opened up and poured out all kinds of imaginative experiences from my own life that helped "the actor" do his work.

Several years into this career, I began wondering if I might be able to harness my self-critic, and my need for perfection, and try writing again. Slowly, I began to realize that much of my difficulty was that I didn't really want to deal with my own intimate, personal feelings on paper. I hid behind perfect beginnings or objective writing. My fears of revealing myself and my childhood pain had stopped me from placing myself onstage in my own work; I still wanted to be invisible, as I had felt when my father died.

I looked around and saw I was not alone. My college writing students as well as my adult school autobiographical writing students were immensely fearful of writing. Most thought they had to learn all the grammar and sentence structure possible before they dared to do any writing. They were terribly afraid of being judged and criticized, either for what they were saying or for the way they were saying it.

Gradually, I began to see a way past all this fear: engaging my students in personal writing as a prelude to academic writing, encouraging them to explore memories from their childhoods before their highly critical, adult selves could take hold. I found that in exploring early memories, my students and I could get in touch with strong images and feelings from the past. The writing of these moments became more and more vivid as we expressed our memories in small, simple, active words and short, powerful sentences. This way of writing seemed to strike close to the heart of the listener, or the reader, who, through the writer's words, was able to see the people in the stories, hear their words, and feel their feelings. The writers appeared quite able to create these stories and at the same time feel safe from the powerful critic in themselves and others. The listeners were touched, moved, and delighted as the writers found their own authentic voices, voices close to the language of modern novels, plays, and movies.

I was delighted to see that many of my students with modest English skills actually did better at this kind of personal writing than did more highly educated students, who had to learn to let go of the impersonal and objective in their writing, which had been hiding all kinds of feelings. I began to reflect on my own life, realizing that for most of it I also hid behind my facility with words, never quite revealing my fears and uncertainties, my embarrassments, my moments of sadness or weakness. "You are not important," my teachers and father had said.

• • •

In the days, weeks, months, and years after my father's death, I was in a great deal of pain. Had a personal writing method, such as the one I have outlined here, been available, it would have helped me a great deal. Large numbers of students come to school every day with the same weighty concerns that I had to deal with as a high-school student. They need to feel that their developing language, writing, and communication skills will help them deal with their feelings and concerns.

The Value of Positive Critique

Writing students need teachers and workshop leaders who approach feedback in a positive way, one that will enhance, not diminish, self-worth. We, as teachers, need to let students know that they are reaching our hearts, not merely our heads, when they write about themselves. They need to know that they have gotten through to us.

Some years ago, a high-risk student of mine wrote a very touching story. She got a lot of positive feedback from the class about the impact of her writing. "It really touched me," was the response of most students. I asked her how it felt to be so well received. "I don't feel so alone," she replied. That single comment made my thirty years of teaching worthwhile.

After Writing Life Stories, Then What?

Once we have acquired some skill in writing stories of our lives, what then? A great many people have a secret desire to create works of fiction—screenplays, novels, short stories, and the like. Is this possible?

Of course it is.

For this reason, I have included in this workbook a number of techniques or steps that I have entitled "Advanced Steps in Writing," which apply to personal writing as well as to the writing of fictional stories.

Just as Leonardo da Vinci created thousands of sketches from life before he did his monumental *The Last Supper* and the *Virgin of the Rocks*, so we as writers can begin our efforts to write fiction by "sketching from life." This is what life stories are—sketches from life. Once we have mastered the art of writing personal stories, then we can begin to paint with a larger brush on a bigger canvas.

———•-•-•———

To develop a fuller understanding of this writing method, you may wish to purchase *Writing from Within: The Next Generation* or *Writing from Deeper Within,* available from Hunter House by calling (800) 266-5592 or by visiting hunterhouse.com.

Readers/writers can participate in an ongoing conversation with the author about life-story writing and the techniques in this workbook. Go to facebook.com/Writing FromWithin. Stories referred to in this workbook and in *Writing from Within: The Next Generation* and *Writing from Deeper Within* are also available at www.WritingFromWithin -Stories.com.

Basic Steps in Life-Story Writing

The following exercises will help you write your stories well. After you have completed them, keep them with you. In the future, you may remember the stories differently. It will be fun to compare.

For starters, ask yourself the following questions:

- How do you feel about writing?
- Has writing been hard for you?
- Do you sense any fears inside you that come up when you face the task of writing?

In this workbook we will talk about any fears you might have so you can identify and handle them when they come up.

Most people are afraid because they think:

1. they won't be able to get their thoughts on paper
2. readers and listeners will laugh at them
3. people will think their work boring
4. they will not be able to finish
5. they will reveal too much of themselves that is painful or may reflect badly on someone else
6. their use of mechanics (spelling, punctuation, etc.) is poor and will embarrass them

Do you feel fearful for any of these reasons? If so, which ones?

_____

_____

_____

_____

There are ways of getting over fear.

One way is to know that all of us, even those who seem very confident, have inside us a critic who corrects everything we do and who can make us feel miserable if we take the criticism to heart. The critic could take on the voice of a parent or a teacher or a boss. It could be the voice of a friend or colleague or someone you don't even know.

Do you remember how, as a child, you could play all day long? Well, you have inside you, as we all do, a creator who wishes to play and create endlessly.

The critic functions to channel the playful energies of this creator into constructive work.

The critic also cautions us about not doing things a certain way—not letting the world see our work unless it is correct and acceptable. Sometimes the critic won't even let us remember our own experiences, fearing that we cannot handle them, and therefore blocks our memories and imagination.

Sometimes this critic's voice drowns out the creator in us.

You need to learn to soften the voice of your critic so you can go on, be creative. Try things out, experiment, and then use your critic's voice at the right time, in other words, after you have finished writing your **first draft.**

If you are like most people, you probably have some difficulty finishing what you start.

You may have an urge to stop after that first paragraph or two to see how you are doing. But when you do this, you lose all your forward momentum, like a base runner who steals second but has to return to first because the batter has hit a foul ball.

When this happens, you get a "what's the use" feeling, don't you?

(This is your critic voice at work, by the way.)

In order to finish what you start, try this solution:

ONCE YOU START WRITING—DON'T STOP.

Run those bases until you reach home plate.

So as you do the exercises in the following chapters, write until you have the picture in your head on the paper.

Then you can look it over; then you can correct your grammar and spelling.

If what's on paper is not what you had in your mind, the following exercises will guide you toward rewriting your story so that it will read better.

chapter 1

Present-Tense Writing

Writing in the present tense forces us to use our imaginations. Small details suddenly become clearer and more vivid in our memories. An additional advantage is that writing in the present tense somehow helps us to get out of our reflective, all-knowing, critical adult self and into a seeing, feeling, more-innocent self.

My Earliest Memory (First Draft)

Your earliest memory is a good place to begin writing because it is something you see in your mind's eye, but it is not too complex to describe. Earliest memories are often dramatic, though sometimes they can be as simple as remembering a shiny thing that hung over your crib. Through these written memories, we have a chance to see what the world was like from the point of view of a child, which is the place where we begin the search for our own artistic voice.

Trigger Your Memory

Think of the first thing you remember in life, at whatever age that might be. Do you have a picture of it in your mind, perhaps even a very vague picture? Picture it even if the memory is just a fragment. It may not be a story at all, just a part of an image. If you are having trouble remembering an early memory, perhaps this list of common experiences will jog your memory.

Topics That May Trigger Your Earliest, Most Vivid Memories

1. my first experience with a birth in the family
2. my first experience with a death in the family
3. my first experience being all alone, without parents or siblings
4. my first experience in the hospital—tonsils out/other illness
5. my first experience riding on a train, boat, bus, or airplane
6. my most vivid memories of Mom or Dad
7. my first day in school
8. my most embarrassing moment in school
9. my first time being really afraid

10. my most vivid memory of my grandparents

11. my first time getting into trouble

12. my best friend in school

Now, (if you are working in a group) tell your story to the others in your group, out loud.

Write Your Memory

Write it down. Start with "I was _____ years old...." For this first draft, tell your story in the past tense.

TITLE: MY EARLIEST MEMORY   (FIRST DRAFT)

"I was _____ years old..." _____

_____

_____

_____

_____

_____

If you need more space, use your own paper. Write "Earliest Memory (cont'd.)" in the top right-hand corner of each page.

My Earliest Memory (First Rewrite)

In the rewriting phase of our work, we can explore using the present tense (using "is," not "was"), which gives the reader a wonderful sense of being present at or in the event. A child knows only what is directly in front of his or her eyes. Therefore, we believe a story written from a child's point of view more easily if it is written in the present tense. We may lose some information, but we gain a great deal in dramatic impact and believability.

Review Your Memory

Begin by telling the first thing you remember again. Tell it out loud to your group or to a friend or a family member, this time in the **present tense** ("I am," not "I was"; "I remember," not "I remembered"; "I do," not "I did").

Shift to Present Tense

What difference do you feel when you tell it in the present tense?

Rewrite in the Present Tense

Now write down what you remember of your earliest memory in the *present tense,* beginning with "I am..." and tell your age when the event happened to you.

Here's an example:

FIRST MEMORY *by Steve Dix*

I am four years old and I am learning to tie my shoe. I keep trying. I have finally done it. Now, I can go tell my mom I've learned to tie my shoe.

From this example you can see that your first memory does not have to be lengthy. It can be very short and still be a good place to begin.

Write it down now.

TITLE: MY EARLIEST MEMORY   (FIRST REWRITE)

I am _____ years old and I am... _____

_____

_____

_____

_____

My Earliest Memory (Second Rewrite)

Writing in the present tense is not easy for some of us. We have been accustomed to writing in the past tense for so long, we can hardly conceive of another way. Yet, writing in the present tense helps to put us in the moment of the events we are writing about and also to create an authentic point of view.

Writing from a child's point of view—stripping your story of adult language—is perhaps the most important consideration for this early story. You may not be able to write exactly as a child would, but you can avoid using vocabulary, diction, and phrasing that a child could not possibly use.

Write in the Present Tense and in the First Person Singular

Review what you just wrote.

Did you write entirely in the present tense? Did you change all your verbs to be **present tense**? If not, go ahead and do so below. What is the difference between writing in the present and past tense?

TITLE: MY EARLIEST MEMORY　　　　　(SECOND REWRITE)

I am _____ years old and I am... _____

_____

_____

The present tense really helps you to be *in* the experience, doesn't it?

T I P **Be sure you write in the first person singular also (not *we* but I).**

My Earliest Memory (Third Rewrite)

The intention of this exercise is to help you sound like you are writing at the age at which the event happened. This is so the reader will have an easier time believing what you are telling them. If, in the earlier example, Steve Dix had said, "I couldn't have been more than four years old when I first tried to tie my shoes by myself," the writing would not have sounded like a six-year-old speaking, would it?

Look over your first rewrite and see if there are any words that sound too old for the age you were in the story. Take out these words or change them.

Go ahead and rewrite now.

TITLE: MY EARLIEST MEMORY　　　　　(THIRD REWRITE)

I am _____ years old and I am... _____

_____

_____

_____

_____

_____

chapter 2

Simplifying Language

When we are young, many things come along that hurt, embarrass, or frustrate us. We soon learn to use language to keep that hurt at a distance…so we won't feel it as we write. As a result, we write in the past tense and use complicated words, anything to avoid reliving the pain of early childhood.

Feedback: Getting It and Giving It to Others

Many students who try to write find it difficult because they feel fearful. It will help you feel good about your work if the thoughts you have about your work or the comments others make about it are not in any way hurtful or critical, as we said in the Preface.

Each of you has an inner voice that can be very hard on yourself. This is the voice of your critic. It may sound a lot like a parent's voice, or like that of one of your teachers. You need to learn to soften the voice of your critic so that you can be creative, and you need to learn where and when to rely on that critic because it often wants you to listen at the wrong time. In other words, it interferes with your creative voice.

It also helps to train your inner critic in what to listen for and what to say. It helps if you can get (and give others) feedback that is not judgmental or critical; that is, not full of *shoulds* and *shouldn'ts* that make you want to stop writing. That way, the feedback will help the part of you that is creative to go ahead and be creative.

The first thing you can do to train your critic is to see if you wrote the first set of exercises in a voice that sounds like a child writing about your life as a child. So, for example, if you wrote about being in school for the first time at six years old, you would want to sound six, not sixteen or twenty-six or sixty.

You can train your critic by giving yourself and others nonjudgmental feedback. If the story was written without complex words and phrases, you might find yourself believing the story more because you are in the story more fully. "I really believed I was listening to a child of six telling her story. I was right there with you the whole time." On the other hand, if the story contained many complex phrases, you might say something like, "The adult-sounding words took me out of the story. I was in it but then I was bounced out, as if I was suddenly watching from a distance."

Using the Voice of a Child

What can you do to sound less grown up? Mostly, it involves taking out certain things from your writing.

Story by a Six-Year-Old

Let's suppose you are twenty-five years old and looking back on a time when you were about six years old. If you were a reader, would you believe this is a six-year-old talking?

> There were times, I suppose, when it seemed as if one would never be permitted to mature at a pace that was reasonable for my age. No, I was forced, albeit in a kindly fashion, to repeat ad nauseam the chores and duties attendant upon childhood: taking out the garbage, playing sports, minding my manners, and obeying the strictures of my parents.

No one reading this passage would suppose for a moment that a child had written it. Why? *Well, children don't talk or write that way.* Let's look at parts of this passage to see what is not childlike about it.

Vocabulary and Phrasing

The following are all phrases no child, other than one attending college at a remarkably early age, would ever use:

"permitted to mature"

"reasonable for my age"

"ad nauseam"

"attendant upon"

Qualifications

Statements that are qualified or modified are virtually never used by children. "I suppose" is a qualification, as is "albeit in a nice way."

The Objective Voice

"One," the objective voice, is virtually never used by children.

Lists

Cataloging chores, etc., in an orderly manner is an adult way of organizing. Children are usually less orderly and logical.

Two Revisions of the Story

Now, let us look at the passage after rewriting it in a way that may not be childlike but at least is not obviously adult.

From the time I was six or seven until I was eleven, my dad insisted that I take out the garbage every Thursday. What a chore that was! It seemed as if he'd never give me any real responsibility, just chores. But I remember one time when he...

Here you have a voice that could be adult or child. The passage is simple and straightforward. The narrator's voice and point of view do not intrude on the action or the progress of the story.

Let's take a final look at the garbage incident rewritten in the present tense:

I am twelve years old. Dad makes me take out garbage every day. Yuk. Every day for six years. "When do I get a chance to do something important?" I wonder.

Suddenly, the story is more intimate, more vivid, more personal. This is the direction we shall pursue for our future stories.

Practice Changing from Adult to Child's Language

Now try out your ability to spot adult language in this story by a young girl. Circle those spots and make the changes that will make it sound more believable as the work of a child.

WILLEM *by Jade*   (FIRST DRAFT)

I have no recollection of the first years of my life. Looking way back into my early childhood, I come up with this little picture, a picture that has surfaced every once in a while whenever I am thinking of the old days.

I must have been three or four. There was a big sprawling backyard. A tall hedge concealed the main house, some distance away. The house was quiet; my mother must be resting. It was siesta time, the time after lunch when the shimmering tropical heat made people drowsy. It was also Sunday, the drone of my father's machines was not there. My father must also be resting. My father had a house-industry at that time. He bought up spices such as pepper, nutmeg, cloves, cinnamon, etc., from the farmers overseas on the other island, then he ground and bottled them in a special building on the grounds. To assist him he asked Willem to come over from his hometown on a far island to work as his foreman. Willem also lived with us in an outhouse.

I liked Willem, because he always spent time with us, whenever there was a chance. That afternoon was no exception. He showed my brother and me some magic tricks and then he said, "Kids, I am going to show you how strong I am!" He asked Joni, another workman, to go fetch the bicycle. Then he lay down on the grass and Joni was told to drive over his chest. I was greatly impressed when Willem stood up unhurt. Then he said, "And now the van will drive over me." Again he lay down on the thick grass and supposedly the car drove over him. I was in awe that nothing happened to Willem. This was where I got befuddled. I am sure I had not told my mother then and there, because she would have taken some action regarding Willem's way of entertaining us and she would have remembered the incident. As it was, when years later I talked about it, my mother said, "Nonsense, he must have tricked you." But I still wonder, did it really happen or was it just my imagination?

If you wish to compare your rewritten version of the story with the way the author rewrote it, here is the author's rewrite:

WILLEM   *by Jade*   (REWRITE)

I am sitting in the grass. The grass is cool and green and very thick and soft; I sink in it. I like to sit there. The sun is very bright, but the hedge behind me makes a shade.

My brother is here, too. He is bigger than I. Papa and Mama are not there. I know they are in the house a little far away behind the hedge. But Willem is there. He is very big, almost as big as Papa. I like him. He always has something nice for me and my brother.

What will he do today? He is lying in the grass. There is also Joni. I do not know him too well, but he does not matter. Willem is there!

Willem is saying, "*Anak mau lihat Willem digiling sepeda?*" ("Kids, want to see the bike run over me?") Joni already goes to fetch the bicycle.

Here he comes straight at Willem lying in the grass. Then the bicycle is already on the other side of Willem and Willem is standing up and laughing. He laughs at us kids. And then, with a laugh in his eye, he tells us that Papa's big truck will now run over his chest. Again he lies down in the thick grass, the car comes and it is over him; only his head sticks out, and he is laughing at us. I hide my head. I am afraid, and I grab my brother's hand. But I still look. Willem is already up again. Willem can do anything!

P.S. Years later when I talked about it, Mother said, "Nonsense, he must have tricked you." But I still wonder, did it really happen?

This rewrite of "Willem" is a much simpler story than the first version, isn't it? This version gives us the feeling of being in the event rather than of watching it from a distance. In fact, we feel as if the event is happening to us, as if we are the child watching the truck go over Willem, wondering how such an awesome thing can happen.

— • • • —

Now go on to your second memory. Remember, these skills can be used to give feedback on your stories or other people's stories too.

Chapter 3

Adding Feelings

"Writing from within" is the act of exploring vivid moments in our lives from the point of view of the age at which we experienced them, and then writing those moments with an intimacy of emotional detail.

My Earliest Vivid Memory (First Draft)

What memory in your life between birth and the age of twelve do you have that is more vivid in your mind than any other, the one that you remember better than any other?

Here is an example of a **vivid memory**:

A NEW SCHOOL   *by Lupe Acosta*   (FIRST DRAFT)

I am eight years old. I'm walking into my brand new school. As I walk into my homeroom, I feel as though everyone is staring at me. I think to myself, "What if my friends get lost and don't meet me at the lockers—then who am I going to hang around with?"

I hope I don't arrive late to any of my classes cuz I'm afraid that the teacher might tell me something in front of the whole class.

The day goes by pretty fast and I have no problems. I finally go home.

Lupe wrote about a very common early vivid memory—a first day in a new school. Other common vivid memories are a birth in the family, a death in the family, a separation or divorce, or a special family event, such as a birthday, a holiday, a trip, or a religious celebration.

Some Vivid Memories

If you are having trouble remembering something vivid, try remembering the first time something happened, such as the first time you went with your father or mother on an adventure, or the first time the teacher told you to behave in school.

Some Vivid Memories

1. An accident happened to a family member or to a friend and I saw it.

2. I made a mistake and was teased by other kids.

3. I was in the hospital getting my tonsils out (or some other sickness).

4. I rode on a train, bus, boat, or airplane, for the first time.

5. I remember some moment about Mom or Dad, happy or sad.

6. Something happened, and I was really afraid for the first time in my life.

7. I remember something vivid about Grandpa/Grandma.

8. I had a good friend in school. Something happened between us.

Now WRITE your earliest vivid memory.

TITLE: MY EARLIEST VIVID MEMORY   (FIRST DRAFT)

I am _____ years old and I am… _____

_____

_____

_____

(Continue on your own sheet of paper.)

My Earliest Vivid Memory (Rewrite)

Now it is time to add another step to your writing. You are going to rewrite your vivid memory and add feelings to your story.

Identify Feelings

Now we will add **feelings** to our story.

Begin by naming as many feelings as you can, based on your experiences now and in the past:

_____

_____

_____

_____

Now, take your perspective at the time of your vivid memory, and identify some of the feelings you recall having in the following situations:

(circle one or two—there is no right or wrong here)

1. In the morning when I get up, I am (happy / sad / anxious / worried / excited) about going to school.

2. When a teacher or my mother or father tells me I have done a good job, I feel (happy / good / surprised / pleased).

3. Whenever my little (brother or sister) hits me, I feel (angry / stupid / ashamed).

4. When my friend hides and then jumps out and says, "Boo!" I feel (scared / surprised / annoyed / angered / bored).

5. I would like to go to college and get a good job. Of course, I know that takes a lot of money. When I think about it I get (worried / depressed / angry / excited / confident / sad).

Feelings in a Story

A story is often about an event happening. The various characters do things to or with other characters. They all have thoughts about what is happening, and they express them. They also have and often express feelings. When a story includes these feelings, the audience can care more deeply about the characters.

If you put feelings into the character who is *you* in the story, the audience will enjoy the story more.

Are My Feelings in My Story?

Ask yourself, "Are my feelings in the story, as I have written it?"

To help, here is a rewrite of Lupe's vivid memory. It was vivid before, but now it also includes feelings.

A NEW SCHOOL   *by Lupe Acosta*   (REWRITE)

I am eight years old. I'm walking into my brand new school. It seems so big and scary. I can feel the butterflies in my stomach as I walk into my homeroom. I feel as though everyone is staring at me. I think to myself, "What if my friends get lost and don't meet me at the lockers—then who am I going to hang around with?"

I hope I don't arrive late to any of my classes cuz I'm afraid that the teacher might tell me something in front of the whole class. How embarrassing.

The day goes by pretty fast and I have no problems. I feel relieved to finally go home.

Do you see how much more interesting the story is when feelings are included? The story sort of pulls us into it, right? It's okay to do more than put your feelings in at the beginning and at the end. Every time an action takes place, bring your feelings into the picture. Remember, it is through your eyes that the audience sees the story.

For the audience to believe what the other people in your story are feeling, the audience has to read the expressions on their faces or figure out what they are feeling from the way they act.

But the audience will believe anything you tell them about how YOU are feeling because they are seeing through your eyes.

After a while you will start to bring your feelings into the story as you write your first draft, but for now adding them in the rewrite is fine.

If your first draft did not include feelings, add them now. As before, begin with "I am…" and tell us your age when the memory happened. Also, be sure it is in the **present tense.**

TITLE: MY EARLIEST VIVID MEMORY (REWRITE)

I am _____ years old and I am… _____

_____

_____

_____

_____

_____

_____

_____

_____

_____

_____

_____

_____

_____

_____

(Continue on your own sheet of paper.)

chapter 4

Brainstorming to Find Stories

To brainstorm about your life memories means to search them out, to let your life memories appear in your mind.

A Second Vivid Early Memory (First Draft)

This is a good time to begin collecting ideas to write about. But if you are like most of us, you probably say, "I don't know what to write about. I can't think of anything."

Let's break down the word BRAINSTORMING into its parts:

The word BRAIN refers to the thing inside your skull where all your THINKING happens. It is to your body what city hall is to a city. All the orders start there.

STORM means to whirl around with great gusts of wind.

So the two parts together connote a whirlwind inside your brain. The word also means to let your thoughts wander around and explore, letting the the pictures in your mind go wherever they wish to go.

Finding the Memories

There are things you can do to make brainstorming easier.

Take a piece of paper, fold it into six parts and tear it so you have six small pieces of paper. Do this three more times so you have a small stack of blank pieces of paper. Now let your mind go back over your memories—the things that are vivid. For each new memory that comes up, write down one or two words on the paper, enough to jog your memory.

For example, here is what I wrote when I was doing this for myself:

BRAINSTORMING   *by Bernard Selling*

1. Dad takes me to see a model train serving hamburgers (write: model train/hamburger)
2. A WWII fighter plane flies over head—I can see the pilot's eyes (write: fighter/eye)
3. Boy next door pins a "kick me" sign on my back after he asks if I want to be the Lone Ranger (write: Lone Ranger)

4. My teddy bear when I was three (write: Kowala bear at 3)

5. My first train set at Christmas. I was four (write: Lionel train at 4)

6. My tongue sticks to the handlebar of my tricycle. I'm three...scared (write: tongue/handle bars)

I went on to do twenty more of these.

Once you have written down these moments, each on one of the little pieces of paper, you can begin to figure out which are "vivid" memories and write those down. Have fun with them. Let the sad ones be sad; the funny ones be funny.

Finding More Memories

When you begin recalling memories, they come faster and faster, like a racer going downhill. You pick up speed. That is the whirlwind part of it.

Also, if you remember one memory, you may remember more things about that memory. In fact, I will brainstorm for a few moments about my father taking me places.

DAD TAKING ME PLACES   (BRAINSTORMING)

1. To Bablo on boat (Detroit River) when I was 5.

2. To Smithsonian Museum, in Washington at 12. Saw Eohippis, size of a hand, first horse.

3. To Railroad Fair, in Chicago, at 12. Got sick.

4. Inside big train engine cab, at 9. Very hot.

5. His office in Detroit, I was 5.

6. To a zoo in Detroit, I was 4.

7. Captured German sub, in Detroit, I was 6.

If you are brainstorming about a parent taking you places, you may wish to brainstorm about how you got to this city. Did you come from another country, another city, another place in this city? Was the trip vivid for you? If yes, you can collect all those vivid moments on your pieces of paper.

Writing Your Vivid Memory

Once you have written down these memories, each on one of the little pieces of paper, you can figure out which are the most vivid and which you want to write about.

Focus on the vivid early memory that happened to you. Make a picture in your mind and then write about it.

Keep in mind the things you are going to do when you write. How do you feel when you write about it? If you feel sad and happy at different times in the story, write those feelings down. Have fun with them. Let the sad memories be sad; the funny ones be funny.

TITLE: A SECOND VIVID EARLY MEMORY   (FIRST DRAFT)

I am _____ years old and I am ... _____

_____

_____

_____

_____

_____

_____

_____

(Continue on your own sheet of paper.)

A Second Vivid Early Memory (Rewrite)

Do you remember the things to do when you are rewriting? Go ahead and rewrite your story. Add any **feelings** you wish to add, change any words that need to be in the **present** tense.

Notice that I ask you to add NEW things in the second draft, not in the first draft. That is because the goal of the first draft is to get it finished, not to make it perfect.

TITLE: A SECOND EARLY VIVID MEMORY   (REWRITE)

I am _____ years old and I am ... _____

_____

_____

_____

_____

_____

_____

_____

(Continue on your own sheet of paper.)

chapter 5

Adding Dialogue

Dialogue is what people say to each other. It usually comes out of vivid emotional moments in the narrative. Adding dialogue in our stories is a powerful way of transcending the gap between the listener's world and the writer's experience. Characters come to life through dialogue.

A Third Vivid Early Memory (First Draft)

Choose a memory of something else that happened when you were young, something that stands out in your mind clearly. Make a picture of it in your mind. Go ahead and write a first draft of this vivid memory. Use the present tense. When you start writing, keep going until you've finished. Don't stop for anything. How do you feel about what is happening? Include your feelings as you write.

> **TITLE: A THIRD VIVID EARLY MEMORY** (FIRST DRAFT)
>
> I am _____ years old and I am . . . _____
>
> _____
>
> _____
>
> _____

A Third Vivid Early Memory (First Rewrite)

Most of us begin to write dialogue quite naturally at the high point in the narrative, which is also the point where we most want the characters to speak for themselves.

Adding Dialogue

Now you are going to add dialogue to your writing. **Quotation marks** ("...") around words tell us someone is speaking those words.

Remember, dialogue makes writing interesting to read. It makes the characters come to life. In the following exercise, I will give you some dialogue and you tell me what kind of a person is speaking. (Circle one)

1. "Gol' darn you, varmint, draw that six shooter if you got the guts," says the old (cowboy in a Western movie / bus driver / school teacher / garbage collector / rock guitarist)

2. "You must not linger any longer on this assignment, boys and girls. Time is up." (cowboy / bus driver / school teacher / pet store owner / congressman)

3. "Four score and seven years ago, our fathers brought forth upon this continent, a new nation, conceived in liberty and dedicated to the proposition that all men are created equal…." (pet store owner / bus driver / a cowboy / a former president of the United States)

From these lines of dialogue you can tell who is speaking and maybe even what they look like, right?

The great thing about dialogue is that it's ok to make it up, although you should try to keep to the truth as much as you remember it.

Often we can create dialogue out of what we have already put down on paper. Here is an example:

> "Mom told me to go to the store" can easily be turned into "Go to the store," Mom told me.

Punctuating Dialogue

Quotation marks and proper punctuation help you indicate who is speaking in a story. For example:

> (")Go get my mirror(,")laughs Cinderella's wicked stepmother. (")I must see if I have grown more beautiful since I last gazed upon myself(.")

Notice the commas and periods inside the quotations marks; for example, "he says," or "she says." Also notice that "he says," "she says," can come after the first phrase in a sentence or at the end of the sentence if it is short. It almost never comes at the beginning of dialogue, at least not good dialogue.

Here are two exercises to help you learn how to use quotation marks and punctuation. Put the proper quotation and punctuation marks in place. There may be more than one mark inside the ( )s.

1. ( )Go home right now( )I tell my sister.
2. ( )Where do I get off the bus( )I ask the bus driver.
3. ( )There must be fifty girls here waiting to try out for the team( )I say to my friend( )Maybe we should just go home( )

Rewrite the next three sentences, turning them into dialogue, using the correct punctuation marks and quotation marks using the following model.

Example: Mom told me to go to the store becomes "Go to the store," Mom told me.

1. Mom tells me to go to sleep.

2. I whisper to my sister that I don't understand why she always teases me.

3. I yell at her to stop hitting me.

1. _____

2. _____

3. _____

Formatting Dialogue

Every time a person enters the scene or speaks, they get a **new paragraph.** In fact, every time a different person speaks in a scene, they get a new paragraph.

Here is an example of what would happen if we had no marks of quotation and punctuation or formatting.

How do you know if I am speaking or you are speaking when writing looks like this I ask my students. It sure is confusing one girl, Janet, answers back. So Mr. Selling tell us, huh? huh? another students says.

Here is an example of what happens when we have the marks of quotation, punctuation, and formatting that we need.

"When a person is speaking, use quotation marks so readers will know he/she is speaking," I tell students.

"How do I know if you are speaking or I am speaking?" Janet, one of my students, asks.

"Each new speaker gets a new paragraph," I tell her. "And put quotation marks around the actual words a person says."

Rewrite the following sentences using the **correct paragraph format,** as well as **quotation marks** and **proper punctuation.** Remember that each new person who speaks gets a new paragraph.

1. There are three girls standing on the corner. I walk up to them.( )Which one of you is Nancy( )I ask them.

_____

_____

2. ( )I'm Nancy( )says the biggest of the three( )Wha'cha' want( )

_____

_____

3. The two cowboys sat down on the bench outside of the marshall's office. Each of them began rolling a cigarette. ( )You seen the marshall( )asks one of them. ( )Nope( )says the other cowboy( )a small mean fella with a scar down his cheek. ( )I think the marshall is a chicken( )says the first cowboy. ( )Mebbe he is and mebbe he ain't( )says the third cowboy, nodding toward the tall stranger walking toward them.

_____

_____

_____

_____

_____

A Third Vivid Early Memory (More Techniques)

Now it is time for you to bring dialogue into your story as you do your first rewrite of your third vivid memory.

   You may not remember exactly what was said but that's okay. You can invent what was said, as long as it feels like the truth. When you have finished writing, ask yourself whether or not your story has been improved by using dialogue.

TITLE: A THIRD VIVID EARLY MEMORY   (FIRST REWRITE)

I am _____ years old and I am… _____

_____

_____

_____

_____

_____

_____

(Continue on your own sheet of paper.)

A Third Vivid Early Memory (Second Rewrite)

Make a picture in your mind of the memory you just wrote about. Did you write it in the **present** tense? If not, rewrite it in the present tense. Did you add your **feelings**? If not, then add your feelings.

   Did you add dialogue? If not, do so now if you can.

   Go ahead and make the changes now.

TITLE: A THIRD VIVID EARLY MEMORY   (SECOND REWRITE)

I am _____ years old and I am... _____

_____

_____

_____

_____

_____

_____

(Continue on your own sheet of paper.)

T I P Don't worry about spelling or grammar when you are writing. After you have finished your story, you can check for errors.

chapter 6

Uncovering Inner Thoughts and Feelings

Inner thoughts and feelings reflect our deepest selves, made visible to others through our writing, giving us a sense that we are completely present in this universe of relationships and unfolding time. Many life experiences block feelings. Writing unblocks these feelings and allows you to move ahead, free and unencumbered.

My Happiest Early Memory (First Draft)

Think of the happiest time you can remember early in your life. Make a picture of it in your mind.

Now write this memory down in the present tense, adding your feelings and dialogue.

You can give it any title you wish.

TITLE: MY HAPPIEST TIME (OR) _____ (FIRST DRAFT)

I am _____ years old and I am… _____

_____

_____

_____

(Continue on your own sheet of paper.)

My Happiest Early Memory (Rewrite)

What questions should you ask yourself to make the story better?

1. Have I… _____

2. Did I remember to… _____

3. Did I remember to… _____

That's right, the answers are 1) written in the present tense, 2) add feelings, 3) add dialogue.

Adding Inner Thoughts and Feelings

Now you can add **inner thoughts** and **feelings** to your happiest memory story.

Here is an example:

> "Go to the store now," Momma says. "I mean now!"
>
> *Oh boy,* I say to myself. *I think I'll call up Martin and he can meet me there and we'll buy some candy.* I pick up the quarter on the kitchen counter. "Yes, momma," I say. "If I really have to I will." *Oh boy, yum, yum.*

These thoughts and feelings from the deepest part of ourselves make a story interesting because they reveal so much about us, allowing the reader to see into our deepest selves.

Now rewrite your memory, adding dialogue and inner thoughts and feelings.

TITLE: MY HAPPIEST EARLY MEMORY (OR) _____ (REWRITE)

I am _____ years old and I am... _____

_____

_____

_____

_____

_____

_____

_____

_____

_____

_____

(Continue on your own sheet of paper.)

chapter 7

Writing Thumbnail Sketches

A thumbnail sketch is a brief clear picture or sketch of a character in our story. In just a few sentences, the thumbnail sketch can tell the reader a lot about that character and also something about the writer—for example, what the writer notices and how observant the writer is.

My Funniest Memory (First Draft)

Think back to the funniest thing you remember in your life. Do some brainstorming, using the pieces of paper to find the funniest moment. Who is in the picture with you? Write their names down here. (If you can remember, give names or a physical description such as hair color or something like that.)

_____

_____

_____

Try to write a story with people in the picture with you.

TITLE: MY FUNNIEST MEMORY (FIRST DRAFT)

I am _____ years old and I am... _____

_____

_____

_____

(Continue on your own sheet of paper.)

My Funniest Memory (Rewrite)

Thumbnail sketches—clear, vivid pictures of the characters—are important so the reader can see what is happening. Here are some examples:

1. The tall stranger comes toward me. He has a mean smile on his face.

2. Melissa is chubby, her fat cheeks always stuffed with food.

3. My dad has bushy eyebrows. They go up in the corners. It makes him look a little crazy. He is always laughing.

What people do helps the audience get a picture of them. Here are some examples:

1. He sat in the corner kicking the chair in front of her. (bored or angry)

2. She looked out the window rubbing her hands together. (cold, worried)

Try Some Thumbnail Sketches

Now try some thumbnail sketches of your family members, using their looks, expressions, size, actions.

1. My brother (or sister), _____, _____

_____

_____.

2. My father (mother), _____, _____

_____

_____.

3. My friend _____, _____

_____

_____.

Now rewrite your funniest memory. Yes, write in the present tense, including feelings, thoughts and dialogue, using quotation marks. Put in a thumbnail sketch if you can.

TITLE: MY FUNNIEST MEMORY   (REWRITE)

I am _____ years old and I am... _____

_____

_____

_____

_____

(Continue on your own sheet of paper.)

Chapter 8

Locating the Beginning of the Story

Don't worry about starting off your stories with a perfect opening when you are writing your first draft. *Finding the beginning is strictly a rewriting task.*

My Greatest Adventure (First Draft)

We start by writing a first draft of another memory. This time write a memory of your greatest adventure. Use the *present tense* and *include feelings, dialogue,* and some *inner thoughts and feelings.*

TITLE: MY GREATEST ADVENTURE (FIRST DRAFT)

I am _____ years old and I am... _____

_____

_____

_____

(Continue on your own sheet of paper.)

My Greatest Adventure (Rewrite)

Now that you have written your memory, see if you have included your feelings, have written in the present tense, and have some dialogue and inner monologue.

Finding the Beginning of the Story

Now let's look at another step in the process. It is called *finding the beginning of the story.*

Step 1

Often, we don't know how to begin our stories. We think that we have to have a great beginning and, if we don't have one, then we can't write the rest of the story. Is that the way you feel? Don't worry about the beginning until you have finished a draft or two.

When you have done all the other things to make your story easy to read and interesting, such as adding dialogue and adding inner thoughts and feelings, then you can work on the beginning.

Step 2

A good way to begin a story is with *dialogue* or *action.*

Look for the first place you have written dialogue or action in your story. Can you bring it up to the beginning of the story? If you can, it may make for a good starting point.

Here is an example:

FIRST DRAFT

I am about 4 years old. My family is going to a friend's house and they have a dog. "I want to pet the dog," I tell my mom.

"Sure, I'll go with you," she says.

"Now, be careful," she warns when we get there. I pet him a couple of times with mom nearby. She sits down again.

"Can I pet him alone?" I ask.

"Sure," my mom says.

When I approach the dog, he bites me on the lip.

Now see what happens when the writer puts the first two lines of action or dialogue (in this case dialogue) in front of the opening narrative ("I am four years old.").

SECOND DRAFT

"I want to pet the dog," I tell my mom.

"Sure, I'll go with you," she says.

I am about 4 years old. My family is going to a friend's house and they have a dog.

"Now, be careful," she warns when we get there. I pet him a couple of times with mom nearby. She sits down again.

"Can I pet him alone?" I ask.

"Sure," my mom says.

Suddenly it becomes a better, more interesting beginning, doesn't it?

Step 3

After beginning your story with some **action** or **dialogue and action,** you may want to bring some factual information into the story later on in the first paragraph or even in the second paragraph.

This is what we call **backstory.** (For more on backstory see Chapter 15.)

TITLE: MY GREATEST ADVENTURE (REWRITE)

I am _____ years old and I am... _____

_____

_____

_____

_____

_____

_____

_____

_____

_____

_____

_____

_____

_____

_____

_____

_____

_____

(Continue on your own sheet of paper.)

> To ask the author questions about "Locating the
> Beginning of the Story" or to share your own thoughts,
> you can join the ongoing conversation at
> facebook.com/WritingFromWithin.

chapter 9

Finding The Climax — Sharing an Intense Experience

One of the things you can do to make a story interesting is to find the climax of the story and expand it, making it fuller, deeper, richer. The climax of a story is the point toward which all the interest and emotion build. It is the point of greatest tension and greatest interest. It is probably what you remember most vividly.

An Experience with Someone (First Draft)

Write a story about the most vivid experience you remember sharing with someone. It may be an argument or an intense discussion or something you did together. Use all the techniques we have discussed so far, but *do not try to create a good beginning in this first draft. Leave that to the second draft.*

TITLE: AN EXPERIENCE WITH SOMEONE   (FIRST DRAFT)

I am _____ years old and I am . . . _____

_____

_____

_____

(Continue on your own sheet of paper.)

An Experience with Someone (Rewrite)

Check your work to see if you have written in the present tense, added your feelings, and have written some dialogue. If not, go ahead and do these things.

TITLE: AN EXPERIENCE WITH SOMEONE   (REWRITE)

I am _____ years old and I am . . . _____

_____

_____

_____

(Continue on your own sheet of paper.)

Expand the Climax of the Story

The climax is where the feelings inside the reader are really strong, usually where there is conflict, struggle or effort, which gets more and more intense until it reaches a breaking point like water boiling in a pot. When the water gets hot, it turns to steam and expands. Soon it boils over. It has reached a climax.

Here is an example:

> One day my brother comes home. He is in a bad mood. He sits down in front of the t.v. I am doing my homework. He tells me to go to the store and buy him some cigarettes. I tell him I have to do my homework.

At this point, we have conflict, which is the point where one person wants one thing and another person another wants something else. As the two people dig in, neither willing to give in, the story builds toward a climax.

> I tell him I have to do my homework. I ignore him. He yells at me some more. I keep ignoring him, hoping he'll get tired.

When we get the sense that someone is going to win or lose, fail or succeed, that is when we know we are at the climax of the story. The climax is what we want to expand in the story, making sure the reader can see the conflict fully and completely.

Now look at the conflict:

> He tells me to go to the store. I tell him I have to do my homework.

This is the part we can expand. What techniques do we use?

1) _____

2) _____

3) _____

4) _____

Here is the conflict expanded at the climax of the story using dialogue, feelings, actions, and inner thoughts.

MY BROTHER JAMES

"Go to the store," my brother, James tells me. "I want some cigarettes." He is sitting in front of the television set at my mom's house with a beer in his hand. I don't look at him. I just keep doing my homework. "I said, 'Go to the store. I want some cigarettes.'"

"I can't," I say. "I have to do my homework. Momma told me to stay here and just do my homework. No matter what." I still don't look at him.

"Huh! You do what momma wants, but you won't do what I want. Is that right?" I turn to look at him. His face is all red and his eyes are crazy looking. "Maybe I should just leave. That would serve you right. I'll just leave. That would serve you right," He laughs, sort of crazy.

"What would momma and me do if he left. We don't got a father and mom doesn't make enough to support us. It scares me to think about that." I keep trying to do my homework. "Maybe I should do what he wants."

He gets up goes in the kitchen.

So far, the story is getting interesting right? The brother wants one thing which is _____. The child wants another thing, which is _____. The brother is trying to get what he wants by doing what? _____. The child is trying to get what he wants by, first _____ the brother then by _____ _____.

The story can now go in one of two directions. If the brother isn't very understanding, the conflict could get worse:

He gets up and goes into the kitchen. I am kind of scared. He comes back with another beer. "Look kid, you do what I say in this house, you understand?" I nod my head. He pushes the back of my head kind of hard. "You go outside and stay out 'til you decide to do what I tell you." I sit in my chair, afraid.

"Go on, out!" I get up and take my jacket. It's cold outside. "You leave that jacket here. You have a lesson to learn," he says. His eyes are hot and mean looking. I go outside and sit on the stairs. I am getting colder, but I won't get him his cigarettes. He is not going to get the better of me.

If the brother is basically a good person who is just a little tired, the story might sound like this:

He gets up and goes into the kitchen. I am kind of scared. He comes back in a moment with a smile on his face.

"I'm sorry, kid. I'm just in a bad mood. I had a bad day. He gives me a punch in the arm and smiles. "Go do your homework."

That would be a happy ending: While he is at the refrigerator, the brother realizes he is being very hard on his younger brother and apologizes for being so self-centered.

Here we have two different ways the climax of the story could go. We have used *dialogue, inner thoughts and feelings,* and *actions* to expand the climax of the story. Can you see more of the picture this way? Do you get more of the child's feelings?

The following is another example of a story in which the climax has been expanded.

TANK TOP   *by Liz Kelly*   (EXCERPT)

"Liz, there's something wrong," Lori says. She puts her arm around me and guides me into the counselor's office. Mr. Cothern, the counselor, gives me a knowing look. I've been here before. Lori sits me down in a chair and I put my face in my hands and cry.

This is where the first draft originally ended. The following paragraph continues the story, expanding the climax to this story.

> Lori leaves to go to class and Cothern and I go into discussion.
>
> "I can't live with my father anymore," I tell Cothern. "I can't handle it."
>
> Cothern gives me a serious look. Well, as serious as his looks ever get. Mr. Cothern is a tall man that reminds me of a character out of a cartoon strip. His eyes are always laughing and I don't think he takes me seriously.
>
> "Cothern, I'm serious." I try to convince him.
>
> "Liz, your dad isn't going to move out, and if you stick around things are going to get better. You can work them out."
>
> "Fine," I say.
>
> I sit and listen a while longer then I go back to class. I know, only too well, that things are not going to change.
>
> P.S. I began to see that my father wouldn't change so I had to. I dropped out of school and moved to Los Angeles from Wyoming. On my day off, I took Mr. Selling's writing class.
>
> I sent my stories back to my family. They began talking about all the things that had happened in the family. My father's rage and the alcoholism that triggered it were part of the discussion. They've been getting help.

(Please see page 114 for the entire story.)

> To ask the author questions about "Finding the Climax —
> Sharing an Intense Experience" or to share your own thoughts,
> you can join the ongoing conversation at
> facebook.com/WritingFromWithin.

chapter 10

Additional Writing Assignments

Little by little, we will find 'writing from within' to be a process that propels us through time and space toward an experience of ourselves that brings the past into the present, allowing us to see ourselves in a multitude of ways. The more we explore these old parts of ourselves through writing, the closer we come to finding our own authentic writing voice, to stepping out onto the center stage of our own lives, and to taking our journey of self-discovery in an unusual direction.

An Experience of Separation

During the process of maturing, each of us experiences a separation from our parents. We become independent and self-sufficient. This is a long, slow process for many people. There are moments that mark the beginning of the process, where we sense we are becoming apart from our parents. It may be reflected in a momentary act of defiance or it may be a moment when we simply feel self-sufficient or independent. But these moments are important.

Write Your Experience

Write about a vivid experience in your mind in which you found yourself feeling separated from your parents or from those who raised you. What was it like? What did you do?

Use all the techniques we have discussed to make the moment as vivid as possible including finding and expanding the climax.

TITLE: AN EXPERIENCE OF SEPARATION

I am _____ years old and I am... _____

_____

_____

_____

_____

(Continue on your own sheet of paper.)

Add a Postscript

Sometimes a moment in your life will have a great impact on you. Not only will you remember it vividly, but it will make an impression on you for a long time to come. Sometimes you will not understand that impact until you have written the story.

It is often a good idea to add a P.S. (postscript) to the end of your story, making clear to yourself what impact that moment had on your life. Notice in Liz Kelly's story "Tank Top" in the previous chapter, she added a P.S. at the end of her story. It was a reminder to herself of the path she had followed, in order to make her life a little clearer to herself. Here it is again:

> P.S. I began to see that my father wouldn't change so I had to. I dropped out of school and moved to Los Angeles from Wyoming. On my day off, I took Mr. Selling's writing class.
>
> I sent my stories back to my family. They began talking about all the things that had happened in the family. My father's rage and the alcoholism that triggered it were part of the discussion. They've been getting help.

Go ahead and rewrite now, adding a P.S. about the impact that moment had on your life.

TITLE: AN EXPERIENCE OF SEPARATION   (POSTSCRIPT)

_____

_____

_____

_____

(Continue on your own sheet of paper.)

Particularly effective in the P.S. is information you wish the reader to know about the experience's effect on the rest of your life. For example, if you detested spinach in the story and you never again ate spinach, the reader will probably enjoy knowing about this.

When you have finished your rewrite, *edit* your story. That means check your *spelling*, your *grammar*, and your *punctuation*. Remember you can use any kind of language you want in your dialogue, but you do want to spell and punctuate it correctly.

An Experience of a Family Relationship

At this point you have learned most of the techniques you will need in order to "write from within" yourself. You may now begin more complex assignments and more interesting ones as well.

Writing from More than One Perspective

Your first assignment is to pick a moment you shared with someone in your family and write about that moment from your point of view.

TITLE: A FAMILY RELATIONSHIP EXPERIENCE

I am _____ years old and I am... _____

_____

_____

_____

_____

(Continue on your own sheet of paper.)

After you have written your story, you may want to ask the other person in your family to write about it from their point of view as well. Do not write for the other person and do not let them look at what you have written before they do the exercise.

After each of you has written, read the other person's story. You will probably see that each of you has a different view of the moment. Accept the difference and do not debate who is right.

Try to get some feedback from others in your family about the two versions of the "truth"—not about who is right but about how differently you each see the moment. See Unit III, "Family History and Explorations," starting on page 81 for more about this process.

A Letter to Mom or Dad

On a separate piece of paper, write a letter to your parents explaining your feelings toward them. Are you angry with them for anything? Sad? Happy? Confused? Hurt? Tell each one in a separate letter. Recall two or three experiences that have caused you to feel the way you do.

You can do this whether or not your parents are alive. It is up to you whether you want to share the letters with anyone, including your parents.

NOTES

_____

_____

_____

_____

_____

_____

_____

_____

_____

_____

_____

_____

_____

_____

_____

_____

_____

_____

_____

_____

_____

Advanced Steps in Writing
Life Stories and Fiction

chapter 11

Using Short Sentences

Once you have mastered the basic steps of "writing from within," you are able to write a very credible story. The present tense brings the story into sharp focus. Simplifying the language reaches the reader's heart and gut. Feelings glue the story to the reader's heart. Dialogue brings relationships to life. Inner thoughts and feelings bring us even closer to the central character. Beginning the story with action or dialogue brings us into the story immediately.

Now we want to focus on several other things you can do to give the story even greater impact. For one thing, you can write short sentences, often dropping the subject and verb in the sentence. This increases the pace of the story without losing clarity. Then, as you begin rewriting you want to sharpen up the characters' qualities: Every action a character takes in pursuit of what he wants comes from a quality he has. Finally, in the second paragraph (more or less), you have an opportunity to slow down the action and give the reader a glimpse of what has gone on before the story opens—what battles, resentments, quirks of fate, and foolish actions have shaped the main character's life.

Using Short (and Incomplete) Sentences

Where possible, you want to use short sentences, especially in the narrative. Allowing the reader to see what is going on, rather than telling them what is happening, moves the story along more quickly.

Here is an example from one of my students, Dale Crum, of effective use of short sentences in the narrative at the beginning of a story. "Smoke Rings" begins with action, transporting us to another time and place, at least for the moment (see the complete text of this story on page 117).

> My cigarette smoke drifts towards Mama's open bathroom window. I smoke two packs of Camels a day and crave nicotine early. Sunshine splashes on the pink shower curtain. Multicolored gold fish fluoresce among its folds.

The second paragraph continues to use short sentences:

Reminds me of tame Calicos, orange Orandas, and Bubble Eyes in the Marshall Islands. They swam close to my navy face mask in the coral reefs only three years ago. Wish I were there, now. These rainy Seattle streets depress me.

This paragraph, which gives us a glimpse of what happened before the story opened, is called *backstory*. The short sentences enable us to get a quick, vivid picture of what is going on in the character's mind as well as what takes place around him.

Here is another example of the use of short sentences that often drop the subject and even the verb of the sentence.

THE BOARD   *by Sam Glenn*   (EXCERPT)

I'm leaving for college tomorrow. Freshman year. Leaving home. Gotta go through my things.

"Sam, I think I'll set up my sewing machine in your room." Mom's voice sounds like she might start crying as she leaves my room and heads to the kitchen.

What to throw away? What to take with me? What to store?

The short sentences in this opening give a punch to the writing. Sam uses incomplete sentences—"Freshman year…leaving home…"—which add more immediacy to the writing. This approach to writing lends itself to a sensation of our being in the presence of someone who is youthful and energetic—a no-nonsense person. In this way, the style of writing short, immediate, sometimes incomplete sentences—conveys a sense of the character's qualities as well as moving the story forward at a rapid pace, which is especially appropriate in a story such as this.

— • • • —

Using one of the stories you have already written, try writing some of the action and the narrative of the story without using complete sentences, just as Dale and Sam do.

First write the sentence as you would ordinarily, then eliminate the subject and the verb. Does this help your story?

TITLE: MY STORY   (FIRST DRAFT)

I am _____ years old and I am… _____

_____

_____

_____

_____

_____

_____

_____

_____

_____

(Continue on your own sheet of paper.)

Using the same story, or perhaps a different one, try dropping the subject and verb in some of the dialogue. It may help give a tone or color to a particular character.

TITLE: MY STORY   (REWRITE)

I am _____ years old and I am... _____

_____

_____

_____

_____

_____

_____

_____

(Continue on your own sheet of paper.)

- -

(T)(I)(P) You will be able to use this technique with some characters but not with others.

- -

chapter 12

Applying the Objective Correlative

Writers sometimes make the mistake of asking an audience or a reader to believe a high state of emotion in a character during the concluding section of a story when the reason for that high state of emotion has not been planted in the beginning of the story.

An *objective correlative* (a phrase made famous by T. S. Eliot early in the twentieth century) is the presence in a story of an object or incident which causes a corresponding emotion in the person most affected by this object or incident.

For this object or incident to be effectively presented in the story, it must also be orchestrated in such a way as to be present in a character's list of concerns, worries or thoughts. That is to say, it must be a defining motif that has been planted in the beginning of the story and is then developed throughout the story.

A good example of a well-placed motif (an objective correlative) appears in David Lean's classic film *Dr. Zhivago.* Midway through the film, Lara is about to leave Zhivago—for him, a searing departure. The music ("Lara's Theme") swells.

Do we know why her departure means so much to him? Indeed we do. In the beginning of the film, a young Zhivago stands at the grave site of his mother as her coffin is lowered into its grave. Zhivago's sense of longing and loss are echoed in the music that swells upward ("Lara's Theme") and a panoply of flowers and snow drifts upward, along with the spirit of Zhivago's mother. So when we witness Lara about to leave, and we see the sunflower in the corner of the frame, and we hear "Lara's Theme," we understand that Zhivago is experiencing profound loss—of his mother, as well as Lara—in this scene. In this way, the objective correlative plays a huge part in our experiencing Zhivago's feelings.

In Dale's story "Smoke Rings" (see the complete text of this story on page 117), the writer provides us with numerous examples (objective correlatives) for his suspicions that he ought not to trust Elsie—she is too naïve. Her smoking is a tipoff that she is young, inexperienced and hungry for experience. Later, when she throws out the ashes, she reveals herself as "gauche," like Dale at an earlier time. Then when she plows through the mud, we see that she is messy. So, inexperienced, gauche, and messy—not a woman for Dale to trust. Of course, the pleasure of the story—the "aha"—the epiphany—is that she reveals herself as far more calculating and aware than Dale ever expected.

— • • • —

Look over one of the stories you have written and ask yourself if you can find a situation where one of your characters is responding with considerable emotion to an incident or object in the story.

Now describe, from the story, the incident that is causing your character to have such a powerful emotion. (For example, a character responding to the death of a loved one in the story.)

_____

_____

_____

_____

_____

_____

_____

_____

_____

_____

_____

(Continue on your own sheet of paper.)

Finally, ask yourself, "Is this incident clear in the minds of the reader?" That is, can the reader understand and feel the same feelings that the character is going through? If not, can you make the incident (the objective correlative) stronger—at least strong enough that the reader can feel these same emotions?

———•••———

Go through all the stories you have written so far and locate characters who are responding and reacting very strongly to an event or incident in the story. Ask yourself if the incident to which the character is responding is strongly enough written so that the reader will understand and feel the feelings of the central character.

chapter 13

A "Hitchcockian Recap"

Alfred Hitchcock, the director of such notable films as *The 39 Steps, North by Northwest, Rear Window,* and *Psycho,* created any number of techniques in his films to keep the viewer glued to his or her seat. One of the most effective was his use of the "recap"—that is, a retelling of what has happened in the film up to the moment when the recap begins. However, this recapping of the events is not mere exposition, but a subtle reviewing of what had happened mixed into a relationship moment.

In a famous and oft-quoted moment in *Rear Window,* James Stewart—an invalid with a broken leg—has been watching what happens in an apartment building across the courtyard from his place. He sees Raymond Burr argue with his wife and then she seemingly disappears. Stewart tells a stunning Grace Kelly—the love interest in the film—his suspicions. She poo-poos his observations and then goes out to run errands. While she is out, a number of significant, intriguing things take place across the courtyard, filling Stewart with dread, concern and worry. When Kelly returns she asks him what has happened, if anything.

Stewart recaps what has gone on in her absence. Kelly, on the other hand, is far more interested in nudging their relationship forward so while he talks, she moves seductively toward him. In a big point-of-view close-up, we see this gorgeous, alluring face of hers moving in to kiss him. Sitting in our seats in the theatre, we are far more interested in her wants and desires than in his pedestrian recap.

Nevertheless, Hitchcock accomplishes his goal: reminding the audience what has happened in the story up to that point in the picture. He uses this technique over and over in his films, always with good results. We may not be aware that information is being fed to us, but the recap tells us just what we need to know so that we will not be lost in any way. (This is also an excellent example of dialogue/action of one character working at cross-purposes—a concept discussed further in Chapter 20—with the dialogue/action of another character.)

This technique is one that we can use in our stories as well. In another story by Dale Crum, titled "My Sister's Shadow" (see the complete text of this story on page 120), Dale meets up with his friend, Milt, and recaps what has gone on in the story, from Dale's point of view. Milt has a totally different take on what Dale has observed. Without the recap from Dale's point of view, the story would not have a great deal of impact. Dale's use of the recap solidifies our grasp of what has happened and, at the same time, leads to a relationship moment when Milt hits Dale with a totally different way of looking at what Dale saw in his sister's actions.

— • • • —

Look over the stories you have written to see if you can find a fairly long story. If you can find one, read it over once or twice. Are you asking the reader to remember a lot of information about the circumstances of the story? About the backstory? About the character's past?

Can you find a place in the story, perhaps around the middle, where a character or the narrator of the story can sum up what has happened so far in the story?

Are you able to find a graceful way of doing this recap, perhaps remembered earlier events during a trip or enjoying retelling these events to another character in the story? Sometimes it is very effective to allow a minor character to do this retelling, such as a dying parent reliving the events of the major character's childhood in a final meeting between the two.

From time to time, you can also have several characters recap what has gone on in the past, each from their own point of view—which will often result in a widely different view of what has happened.

If you can find such a moment, write it in the space below, then rewrite it until it feels like a natural part of the story.

_____

_____

_____

_____

_____

_____

_____

_____

_____

_____

(Continue on your own sheet of paper.)

chapter 14

Developing Character Qualities

How a person goes about getting what he or she wants reveals certain character qualities. Charm, determination, humor, honesty, self-assurance, dependability, opportunism, and perfectionism are all qualities that get us what we want; they may also, tragically, defeat us in other ways.

One of the most important aspects of creating stories is developing interesting characters. When we look at a dramatic film, such as *On the Waterfront* with Marlon Brando, we find ourselves caring about the characters to the degree that we see them struggle against great odds to attain something they care about. The more they care, the more interesting, the more fascinating, they become.

How they go about pursuing their dreams, their comeback, their goal is what we care about in a story.

Are Character Qualities Evident in the Story?

For character qualities to shine through your story, each character must know clearly what they want. Yes, these wants may change as the story progresses, but for character qualities to emerge from your pages, each character must have a clear sense of what they are pursuing. Such a goal may be further defined as the *character's intention.*

For a story to work, every major character must face a significant obstacle to achieving their goal (intention). Gripping drama ensues when a character tries to overcome an obstacle using qualities that have worked in the past, qualities that don't work in the present, so the character must find other qualities (and take other kinds of actions) in themselves in order to achieve their goal (intention).

Every action that a character takes stems from the **character qualities** they possess, even though the character may not know they possessed those qualities in the beginning of the story.

Examples of basic character qualities that get us through life are: honesty, humor, dedication, adaptability, persistence, ingenuity, and passion.

For example, in *On the Waterfront,* Brando's character has been knocked around the ring for so long, he doesn't think all that straight. When his brother, who hangs out with the local mob run by Johnny Friendly, tells him to do something thing, he does it, no questions asked.

But when he encounters an upstanding woman (Eva Marie Saint) whom he desires, a woman who wants to find her brother's killer, the Brando character finds himself torn between loyalty to his brother and the mob and loyalty to this woman with whom he has fallen in love. The character quality that fights to surface is *emotional honesty*. He may not tell her the whole truth in the beginning but he doesn't lie to her. Finally he admits he knows who killed her brother…and even that he had a small part in the killing. He risks her rejection in favor of telling her the truth about his involvement. Later, he risks his brother's love by going to the government with evidence against the mob.

The first obstacle the Brando character faces is Eva Marie Saint's goodness—her virtue. At first, to win her love he tries to bring her into his life—dancing at a bar—and uses his charm to win her interest. It doesn't work. Gradually, he finds that he must develop other qualities that have been dormant in him for a long time: honesty and responsibility.

(**Note:** If you are interested in knowing more about character qualities, a more in-depth discussion of this concern may be found in my book *Character Consciousness*.)

In writing a story, whether fictional or nonfictional, we need to write the first draft in whatever way we would ordinarily do so, without concerns such as, "Are the characters' qualities visible?" However, from the second draft on, sharpening these qualities becomes a primary concern for us. For example, those actions that a character takes to get what they want in the development section or the concluding section of our story, must be planted as a motif, in the "setup"—the introductory section—of our story. Generally speaking, writers get into trouble by having characters take actions, late in the story, that are not suggested in the setup of the story.

When done well, character qualities yield a sense of knowing a character well, of being able to anticipate how they will handle a situation and whether or not he will find new qualities in himself to handle new obstacles.

— • • • —

Select one of your stories and examine the actions that character takes in pursuit of what they want. Ask yourself, what does this character want? If you know with great clarity what the answer is, then ask yourself, "What character qualities does my character exhibit?"

I suggest you write out what the character wants at the beginning of the story and what character qualities they need to get what they want. Do the same for the character at the development section of the story and at the concluding section of the story.

TITLE: _____

SETUP (INTRODUCTION)

Character (name): _____

Goal: _____

Character qualities: _____

_____

DEVELOPMENT SECTION

Character (name): _____

Goal: _____

Character qualities: _____

_____

CONCLUSION

Character (name): _____

Goal: _____

Character qualities: _____

_____

I suggest you do this for each of the important characters in the story.

If the qualities of your important characters differ from one section to the next, that is a good thing. It suggests that your character is discovering different aspects of himself as the story progresses. Check your story to be sure that some aspect of the character qualities to be found in the conclusion may be found in a small way in the two earlier sections.

This exercise may be used before you have written your story or after you have written your first draft. The goal here is to find ways of checking the clarity of your characters once they are down on paper.

Do not allow this analytical work to stop you from writing.

— • • • —

One of the most effective ways of employing character qualities is to have a minor character hit a central character with a negative quality early in the story. The ensuing drama will then become a story of the central character's efforts to disprove the definition (which in all likelihood is true). Here are some examples:

Drill Sergeant: "I want all you lily-livered, namby-pamby city boys to show me some grit…true grit." (Note: In the movie *City Slickers,* the Jack Palance character speaks to Billy Crystal in a similar way.)

Elaine Stewart to John Wayne in *Red River:* "You need a woman by your side at night…to bring softness and comfort to your life" (i.e., stop being so stubborn and manly and allow a woman into your life).

Select a story that you have already written and look for a place where a minor character can *label* or *define* a major character with a definition of a negative quality, such as the John Wayne character's *stubborness* in the above example.

_____

_____

_____

_____

_____

_____

_____

_____

_____

_____

_____

_____

_____

_____

(Continue on your own sheet of paper.)

> **Identifying and developing character qualities is a "life" or "survival" concern, not just a writing issue. To ask the author questions about "Developing Character Qualities" or to share your own thoughts, you can join the ongoing conversation at facebook.com/WritingFromWithin.**

chapter 15

Including Backstory

One of the most effective ways of giving the reader some context to whatever is going on when the story opens, while also giving dimension to certain characters, is to provide some *backstory* to the event that is taking place.

Very often this backstory will occur in the second or third paragraph of the story. The first paragraph will probably be devoted to an "attention getter" that takes the reader out of his boring, humdrum life and thrusts him into a story.

However, in the second or third paragraph, an effective writer will weave some history of what has gone on in the recent or deep past into the unfolding narrative. Here is Dale's second paragraph backstory in "Smoke Rings" (see the complete story on page 117):

> Reminds me of tame Calicos, orange Orandas, and Bubble Eyes in the Marshall Islands. They swam close to my navy face mask in the coral reefs only three years ago. Wish I were there, now. These rainy Seattle streets depress me.

From this we know that the writer is not some rebellious teenager but a veteran of World War II who has acquired habits like those of others his age, along with an urge to move along in life, get educated, make something of himself.

Effective writers will also provide us with backstory as we move through the story rather than giving backstory to us all at once.

In Dale's story, a few more sentences of dialogue reveal that Dale is thinking about leaving his parents' home in Seattle and heading for college in Southern California.

> My B-50 flight control rigger's job only pays one dollar and ten cents an hour. That's union swing-shift wages, too. Boeing hired me a year ago for seventy-five cents an hour. Maybe Harry Truman here in the beginning of his first full term can kick start the peacetime economy.
>
> I sold my 1941 Buick sedan for eleven hundred dollars. Bought a cream puff '37 Chevy sedan for only four hundred. The G.I. Bill will pay for my college tuition. With a part-time job I can have fun in the sun and learn something, too.

Another helpful example occurs in the story "In the Beginning…" by Roy Wilhelm.

IN THE BEGINNING… *by Roy Wilhelm*

The plaque on the wall near the front entrance states this state youth prison was built 10 years ago in 1962. How many times have I looked at that plaque in the last half hour as I paced back and forth? This time as I stop to stare at it, a voice interrupts my thoughts.

"You sure read slow. You've been studying that plaque the whole time I walked through the parking lot from my car."

I quip, "I have bachelor's and master's degrees, but I still read slowly." He laughs. "Actually, I was deep in thought while I wait for my job interview. The receptionist said it will be awhile until they call me. I'm so nervous, I had to take it outside here to get fresh air."

He replies, "Well, it sure is a great place to work. Good luck to you." He walks inside.

Man, I want this job so bad. I'm forty-one years old and for twelve years, I've studied, trained, and had various jobs that would qualify me to be a California state institutional chaplain. Three years ago, they interviewed me, but they hired somebody else. I'm thoroughly frustrated.

My wife and I drove from Phoenix, Arizona and stayed last night at the home of my friend, Rev. Dan Berth. He told me, "Roy, I visited Ventura School in Camarillo a year ago. It's like a high-school campus. I think the Lord made you wait and prepare yourself this long so you'd be well qualified to help those young people." He patted me on the back. "I'm sure you'll get the job."

Notice that the third paragraph describes what has happened in the past, enabling us to understand what getting the job means to Roy, and how much is riding on getting this job; that is, how high the stakes are.

Most effective stories employ backstory to give a rich sense of where the central character has come from, as well as the minor characters. Perhaps they will be called upon to rise above the inclinations of others like them. That is the value of backstory.

—●●●—

Take a look at the stories you have written. Read over the first four paragraphs of your stories. Have you included a second or third paragraph "backstory" that gives the reader a more developed picture of the situation the central character is in when the story opens?

If you have not, try creating a backstory—not necessarily a long one—after your story's opening scene has ended. Or you may wish to interrupt your opening scene to include backstory. When you have finished ask yourself, "Is the story more effective with the backstory included?"

Select one story and write down a possible backstory. If it works—that is if it adds something to the story—then include it.

_____

_____

_____

_____

_____

_____

_____

_____

_____

_____

_____

_____

_____

_____

_____

_____

(Continue on your own sheet of paper.)

You may also wish to include some additional backstory as your story unfolds.

> **It takes a long time to grasp the importance of and to develop skill in building backstory. To ask the author questions about "Including Backstory" or to share your own thoughts, you can join the ongoing conversation at facebook.com/WritingFromWithin.**

chapter 16

Ending with a Denouement

When we look at the ending of a story, we begin to understand the need for something to happen after the climax of the story has been reached. A skilled writer pays close attention to how the story ends in an emotionally satisfying way. Once the climax has been reached, the audience must be allowed to experience a gradual diminution, an untying of the knot of the emotion that has built up on the way to the climax. Aristotle called this release of emotion a *catharsis.* Another term for this release of emotion is called the *denouement*—a French word meaning, quite literally, "untying." Here I use the term in the sense of its being a falling off of energy.

Here is the ending of Dale Crum's story "Smoke Rings." See if you can spot the denouement of the story.

> We reach Los Angeles late the next day. I park in back of the women's dorm, shake out the kinks, and open the trunk. I turn with Elsie's bag and bump into a guy. He hugs Elsie and asks her, "Drive nonstop from Seattle?"
>
> "Nope. Willie, this is Dale," she replies. "Stopped in southern Oregon."
>
> He persists, "Side of the road?"
>
> "Nope. Motel."
>
> She swivels her body away. Willie's face turns color. He slobbers into his red bandana handkerchief. I steel myself for his next question. In the same room?
>
> He makes choking noises. No words come out. They stand nose to nose. I set her bag down, back out of the lot and light up a cigarette before he clobbers me.
>
> I've seen riled up Cajuns in the navy. They hold both hands together in a giant fist and slam down on someone's head. Pole-axed, they call it.
>
> Four days later I sit near Elsie in the cafeteria. She waves her left hand at me. A large rock sparkles on her ring finger.
>
> She giggles, "Me and Willie."
>
> I give her a big epiphany smile of admiration. "Congratulations."
>
> She outsmarted both her mother and me. Made Willie jealous enough to pop the question. I feel relieved. For once I don't need another cigarette. Any more may drive me crazy, may drive me insane.

The climax occurs when Willie shows his emotions at the thought of Elsie and Dale sleeping together. Perhaps Willie will tee off on Dale. The wonderful twist to the climax is the moment when Elsie shows Dale the ring that Willie had just given her. This is the moment of greatest tension…and release. Dale's realization that his take on Elsie had been wrong—that she had not been trying to hook Dale at all—constitutes a satisfying denouement to the story.

—•••—

Look at several of your stories. Figure out—in each one of them—where the climax of the story lies. Is it close to the end of the story? Does the writing from the end of the climax to the end of the story feel as if it ties everything up? Are all the questions that occur in the reader's mind ("How is it all going to end?") answered?

Isolate one such ending and ask yourself if all the questions that may be on the reader's mind are answered by the time you finish the story. Write down all the questions that the reader might be asking as they approach the climax to the story.

_____

_____

_____

_____

_____

_____

_____

_____

_____

_____

_____

_____

(Continue on your own sheet of paper.)

Having raised all these questions, ask yourself if each question has been answered. If not, rewrite your ending so all the questions are answered. Is the story more effective now? Is the final moment a little more graceful?

chapter 17

Creating Three-Dimensional Minor Characters

Examples of sophisticated use of minor characters, visual motifs, and form abound in the work of fiction writers. However, these techniques as used by fiction writers are also available to the writer of nonfiction life stories.

This does not mean that we invent what we need, as does a fiction writer. On the contrary, we learn to see these things happening in life, and in so doing, we begin to see them as part of our stories, not as inventions but as what truly occurs in life. Minor characters throw into high relief the struggle of the central character. Visual motifs underscore the meaning, theme, and plight of the central character. Finally, we want to be sure that any motifs we create—character motifs (actions and the like) or visual motifs—occur in the setup to the story (the first third), that they unfold in the middle, and that every motif pays off at the end of the story. This is what we mean by *form*. For more on form, see Chapter 19.

The quality of our storytelling will become substantially better if we allow minor characters to react to circumstances that bedevil the major characters.

Very often minor characters fall into certain types: the mentor, the playboy, the innocent, the martyr, the trickster, the villain, the mystic, the adventurer, the old wise man, and the like. These types often exist in life and a knowledge of them allows us to see them when they cross our paths.

In Dale Crum's story "My Sister's Shadow" (see the complete story on page 120) we notice that Dale is uncertain about whether he really ought to be trying to protect his sister or not. Therefore, he seeks out Milt, a friend who advises him to let well enough alone. But Milt does more than that. He levels a certain amount of criticism at Dale for being naïve. In doing so, the character of Milt reveals himself to be something of a trickster—an impish, mercurial type of person whose unpredictability serves the main character well by saying things to him that others might not be willing to say aloud.

> "Cleo doesn't go with church guys. Claims they're too sissified."
> [Milt] sneers, "Sounds like what my sisters might say about you, Dale."

The reactions of minor characters often govern the actions of major characters. In motion pictures, such reactions are often vital to the progress of a film.

In the old *Gunsmoke* television shows, Marshall Dillon would inevitably wind up in a gun fight with the bad guys. In and of itself, this might not alarm us, the viewing audience. However, when Chester, Doc, Festus, and Kitty start to react with fear and/or concern, then we begin to do so as well.

Well-developed minor characters deserve the same kind of care in delineating their wants and needs as do major characters. Well-drawn minor characters have an arc that spans the course of the story.

To continue with the example of *On the Waterfront,* Marlon Brando's brother, played by Rod Steiger, is such a character. Early in the movie, he is simply a henchman of the mob's Johnny Friendly. Two-thirds of the way through the film he pleads with Brando to stay in the embrace of the mob. Brando resists. He is now influenced more deeply by the Eva Marie Saint character. In the end, Steiger's character accepts that Brando will go his own way and that it probably means "the end" for Steiger's character, who accepts his fate with quiet finality, and love for his brother.

—— • • • ——

Outline the objectives (goals/wants/needs) of each minor character in your story:

_____

_____

_____

(Continue on your own sheet of paper.)

Outline the adaptations (*how* they go about getting what they want/the actions they take):

_____

_____

_____

(Continue on your own sheet of paper.)

Describe the *character qualities* each minor character has that allows them to take the action they take:

_____

_____

_____

(Continue on your own sheet of paper.)

chapter 18

Creating Visual Motifs

One technique used by writers and filmmakers to underscore messages/themes they wish to impart to the reader is implanting a strong visual image that resonates in the mind of the reader and viewer. This visual image is a type of **motif,** which is simply a pattern of some kind. Motifs work best when they reoccur at least three times, once in each section of the story.

For example, in John Steinbeck's *The Grapes of Wrath,* the Joad family lumbers to California in a beat-up old truck. In the middle of the road, under a hot, desert sun, a turtle moves across the highway, ever so slowly. The Joad vehicle flips the turtle on its back, leaving it to bake under the hot desert sun, unable to right itself. This image of the turtle is the writer's way of giving us a clue as to the fate of the Joad family — a creature struggling to survive, out of its element (the farms of the midwest dust bowl), helpless under the cruel, hot sun.

Writers of life stories can do the same things. All around us, visual things echo the struggles of the central character. To use them as motifs in stories, they need to occur in the setup of our story, then again in the development section and again in the conclusion.

In Dale Crum's story "Smoke Rings," the cigarette is a visual motif that signifies different things. In the beginning of the story, his cigarette symbolizes his independence from his family, his worldliness and impatience with their way of life. In the hands of cute little Elsie, it's an expression of innocence seeking worldliness. Later, Elsie dumps the ashes of her cigarette on the ground, suggesting her unthinking messiness, not a woman whom Dale wants to trust with his well-being. In a similar way, Dale skirts the muddy sidewalk as he approaches the motel office, but Elsie just sloshes her way through the mud, again the symbol of unthinking messiness. Here is what Dale has to say about creating motifs in his stories:

> I don't think "motifs" per se when I start a story. But by the time I write the first page, natural motifs, which were there all the time, pop up in my memory — a cloud, a blue sky, a baby's cry. The feel of her hand. Smells of the river. A taste of honey. Then I add them, starting near the top of the story. They work best when scattered throughout.

Visual motifs are a powerful tool for a writer. If a motif is central to the character's actions, the audience will *feel* rather than *know* the power of the image. For example, in Shakespeare's *Macbeth,* the prophesy—that order will be restored "when Birnam Wood comes to Dunsinane"—plants in our minds the idea of the restoration of order, early in the play. But the audience thinks little about it until the end when McDuff's forces emerge from Birnam Wood, concealed beneath brush from the forest, as they crawl toward the castle of Dunsinane. When Lady Macbeth sees the prophesy coming true, the impact of it comes to her and the audience in a gasp.

Often times, visual motifs gain significant power from their representation of a moral or god-given order in the universe. The turtle struggling to right itself or Birnam Wood coming to Dunsinane suggest a moral order in which the turtle ought to be allowed to right itself and Birnam Wood ought to come to Dunsinane. In an age when the certainty of a moral order is open to question, the presence of powerful visual symbols reassures us that a moral order may exist.

It hardly need be said that one person's moral order may look like tyranny to another person: Witness the varieties of national symbols, such as the swastika, that provoke all kinds of emotion in people. So, at the same time we search for arresting visual symbols in our stories, we also look for the use of ominous symbols that help define nonheroic characters in these same stories; for example, in Shakespeare's *Richard III,* the author refers to Richard III as "weed in the garden."

———•••———

Take a look at several of your stories. Select one to work on. Scan the story to see if you can add a visual motif that you can work into the story through the introduction, the development section of the story, and the conclusion (the summing up/recap/etc.). Dale's use of the cigarette in his story is a good example.

Visual motif: _____

_____

_____

_____

Introduction (describe): _____

_____

_____

_____

_____

_____

Development (describe): _____

_____

_____

_____

_____

_____

Conclusion (describe): _____

_____

_____

_____

_____

(Continue on your own sheet of paper.)

After describing the motif and how you expect to use it in the story, go ahead and include it. Then have several of your readers give you feedback about how effective it is in the story.

If they conclude that your story is more effective with the visual motif included, then look at your other stories to see if you can develop visual motifs in them.

chapter 19

Creating Form

The human mind cannot hold in its memory bank very much of what it receives. Therefore, the artist must create a form (shape) that allows the audience to make sense of and then remember what it receives. In this way, the principle of *repetition* enters the picture for the writer. Most stories have a beginning (called a *setup*), a middle (called a *development*) and a conclusion (sometimes called a *recap*). At the beginning of a story—what we call the setup—motifs are introduced. In the middle third of a story, these motifs are developed. In the conclusion, the conflicts in the motifs are resolved in some way.

Steinbeck introduces the turtle motif in the beginning of *The Grapes of Wrath*. That is, he shows us the creature, upended, struggling to survive under the worst of conditions. In the development section, the members of the Joad family struggle terribly with the poverty into which they have been thrust. In the conclusion, they find ways of coping, of righting themselves, and surviving.

Painters are fortunate. They can create an illusion of three dimensions on a canvas by means of focal point perspective. This is a kind of form that enhances the sense of the illusion of three dimensions. Leonardo da Vinci's *Last Supper* extends the perspective lines of the refectory in which the fresco is housed to create an illusion of Christ's presence. Modern artists are often interested in "design" elements that have a life of their own independent of creating an illusion of three dimensions. Piet Mondrian, who painted with primary colors and horizontal and vertical black-line grids, is one such modern artist.

Writers have a more difficult task. For the most part they are interested in creating an illusion of three dimensions, that is, they want the audience to believe that what they are seeing is, in some sense, real. Yet, at the same time, the writer has to create a sense of form so that what the reader's eye sees coming from the page makes sense and can be grasped by the mind.

With this in mind, the story must have an arc that the reader can follow: A sad circumstance gets worse then gets better (*Stalag 17*; *On the Waterfront*; *Some Like It Hot*), a good circumstance takes a turn for the worse then gets better (*Sullivan's Travels*), a happy but challenging circumstance turns better then ends badly (*Gone with the Wind*), a sad circumstance gets better then turns worse (*Rebel Without a Cause*). In your own life, a vivid memory from each decade will give you a sense of the arc of your life.

Within the story's arc, each major character must also have an arc and fully realized minor characters must each have an arc as well. Dale's story "Smoke Rings" provides us with a nice sense of Dale's arc as well as Elsie's.

Here is Dale's arc:

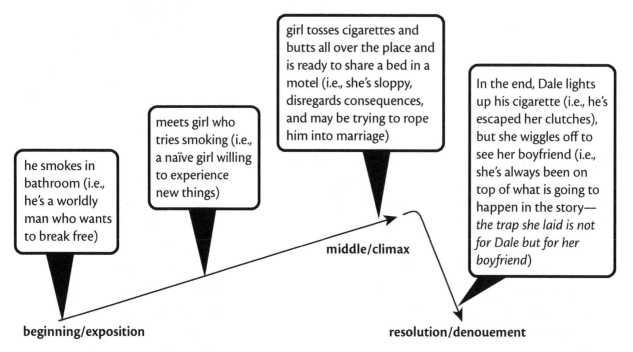

Dale's story arc in "Smoke Rings"

The visual elements of a story, whether a life story, a novel, a short story or screenplay, must also have an arc and must fit into the arc of the story. For example, at the beginning of David Lean's *The Bridge on the River Kwai,* a Japanese train winds its way through the jungle. In so doing, it passes a number of crosses—symbols of the men who have died building the bridge. The camera then comes to rest on William Holden as he pauses while erecting (and resisting erecting) yet another cross. Here all the visual elements come together: building the railroad bridge over the river Kwai, the human lives lost in building the bridge, Holden as a survivor who is going to beat the odds. These are the visual ingredients—the motifs—with which the filmmaker will build the arc to this film.

In certain plays, novels and short stories, the language itself becomes an element in the arc of the story. For example, in James Joyce's *Ulysses,* the writer creates a profusion of allusions to past Irish history, which makes the going difficult for a modern-day, non-Irish reader. Two thirds of the way through the book, the style suddenly changes when the wandering Jewish character, Bloom, comes to a beach (the "Nausicca" section of the book) where a number of young girls play in the water. This sudden lapse into pulp fiction is to show how easily we are all conned into "believing" and getting caught up in language and images that appeal to our senses, just as it happens to Bloom.

Like Brecht, the German playwright and contemporary of Joyce, and Mondrian, the Dutch painter, the artist's aim is both to create something either realistic or bordering on realism, and then to break that sense of realism in order to make the reader or viewer especially conscious of the literary, visual, and aural techniques that may manipulate the reader and viewer as they experience both the work of art and life.

For a more in-depth analysis of the various "arcs" of the different characters in Ernest Hemingway's "The Short Happy Life of Francis Macomber," the reader may wish to take a look at Chapter 11 in *Writing from Deeper Within* and Chapter 30 in *Writing from Within: The Next Generation*.

—•••—

Select one of your stories to work on. Describe the arc of the story.

Story Arc: _____

_____

_____

_____

_____

_____

_____

_____

_____

_____

_____

_____

_____

(Continue on your own sheet of paper.)

This kind of outline can be used to tease a story out of one's imagination or it can be used after a first draft to clarify for the writer the elements of storytelling that become important in the course of telling each story.

chapter 20

More on Narrative, Dialogue, and Inner Thoughts and Feelings

In telling a story, every writer has three essential ingredients to their writing "stew"—narrative, dialogue, and inner thoughts and feelings. The way in which they manipulate these ingredients dictates the style that emerges and the pleasure the audience derives from the story.

We will now take a closer look at some of the techniques we described as "basic" in order to see how we might use them in a more sophisticated way.

Narrative

In Chapter 1, I asked you to tell a story first in the past tense and then in the present tense. Without using the fancy word "narrative," I was asking you to write the story using narrative action, first in the past tense then again in the present tense. This moved the story along in the most vivid, present way possible.

The word narrative is a fancy word for a "story," which might be defined as a relating of facts about a particular episode that unfolds in time and has a shape or an arc that moves the story forward. This "narrative" often moves the story forward without concern for the characters' particular qualities, and the actions that emerge from these qualities.

A more sophisticated unfolding of the narrative may include much more than simply a relating of the facts. For example, if you ask yourself, "Do the details and actions of the character make the story more interesting?" behind this question lies an assumption: A narrative ought to be broken down into something else. Generally, this is true. Here is an example from J. D. Tousley's story "Cricket," which he later turned into a novel, *Dangling in the Adios*:

> My life as a young pool hustler was about as sweet as life gets. In those days, long before MasterCard, when you could sit down at a nice clean lunch counter and get a bowl of steaming chili for a quarter, a slab of apple pie juicier than Mom made for a dime, and a steaming cup of coffee with free refills for a nickel, I usually carried at least two hundred bucks in my right front pocket and a couple of fifties hidden in my wallet. So I was doing all right.

I'm telling you, business life couldn't have been sweeter, played out day by day on a rectangle of green felt four and one half feet wide by nine feet long. And I knew every inch of it.

Now this is good, helpful material. In fact, these two paragraphs are backstory to the story the writer intends to tell. We know it's backstory because he mentions the present: "…in those days, long before MasterCard…."
Here is the story after a few more drafts:

I've had it with stuck-up sorority girls. They act like they're too grand to do it, then when they finally let you in, they own you lock, stock, and barrel. Take Carolyn Forsythe, for instance, safely locked away from us college boys in her panty girdle. After we first met, I rolled around with her in the backseat of my convertible every night for two weeks, trying to pry her out of that medieval contraption, until late one night I got her to wriggle out of it on her own and start enjoying life. And it's been great. I never had it so steady before. But I'm paying for it with my freedom. Whenever Carolyn crooks her finger, I'm supposed to roll over and bark. You'd think she owned me. Now she's ragging me to quit playing nine ball so we can study together. Hell, I don't need study. That's what brains are for. And I'm not about to give up nine ball. Pool is my life, and besides, it brings in about thirty bucks a week.

The writer is still using a narrative style that doesn't include dialogue or inner thoughts and feelings but is nonetheless building up a portrait of the girls in his life—first Caroline the sorority girl, and next Cricket.

How different with Cricket, my appreciative little drugstore clerk. … I met Cricket a couple of weeks ago. She clerks at the drugstore around the corner from campus. One day I went in to buy a comb. Five minutes later, I had a new comb and a new girlfriend. Mostly I take her to drive-in movies and an out-of-the-way beer joint called Snookums in south Kansas City where I won't run into anyone Carolyn knows. Carolyn has gone home to St. Louis for a few weeks during summer break, which gives Cricket and me time to get acquainted.

Nothing's perfect though. Her father doesn't like me and he's getting in my way. Just today Cricket reminded me on the phone that tonight is our seventh date. "Daddy raises Cain if I go steady," she said. "We'll have to find another way to meet before he goes berserk."

Technically, it is not narrative because nothing here moves the story forward—it's still backstory leading to the present-day story the author intends to tell. But it is rich nonnarrative, filled with separate little stories of how the character got himself into this situation, all of it very visual. The character qualities of Carolyn and Cricket abound: controlling, possessive, uptight Carolyn; spontaneous, innocent, carefree, adoring Cricket.

Already the narrative has transmuted itself into little pieces of action and backstory that do not move the story forward, necessarily, but do give a picture of the circumstances in which the central character finds himself. Already he's in a vise and he's being squeezed. As the story progresses, we see that the author brings the characters into greater focus through dialogue and inner thoughts and feelings.

———•••———

Select one of your stories and see if you can enhance the narrative (the story line) by adding discreet character delineation that include backstory, action, and description.

_____

_____

_____

(Continue on your own sheet of paper.)

Dialogue

In Chapter 5 I suggested adding dialogue to make a story better, more interesting, and more revealing of the characters who speak.

However, more needs to be said about dialogue. In the nineteenth century, novels such as those of Dickens, Thackery, Melville, and the like contained long passages of all narrative. Dialogue was sprinkled in here and there. A writer from this era filled his pages with cumbersome narrative and then punctuated the narrative with pungent, expressive dialogue. By the time we get to Fitzgerald in the late 1920s, the characters speak more and more often with less narrative needed to move the story along. In the 1930s and 1940s, we have writers who, like Hemmingway and Steinbeck, express themselves almost completely in dialogue and action.

What is the importance of dialogue? Dialogue is comparable to a two shot (a medium-distance shot that often shows two people) in a motion picture. It provides a strong sense of relationship between or among characters. Deft film directors using modern, light cameras and dollies recompose the frame of their films so that long shots, medium shorts (two shots), and close-ups occur within a single take. Writers do the same thing, often including within a series of paragraphs, the setting of a scene, dialogue, and inner thoughts and feelings of the major character, and sometimes minor characters, as well.

Vivid Dialogue

The most vivid stories that we read or see on screen as films and television programs often have vivid dialogue. A number of ways exist to create interesting dialogue. Perhaps the simplest way to create vivid dialogue happens when you *eliminate the subject and/or the verb from the sentence.* Here is an example from "Smoke Rings." Let's look at the first line of dialogue from Dale's story:

> "Stunt your growth," my dad used to say.

In this case, Dale dropped both the subject and part of the verb: "It will…" The sentence becomes more effective because a lot of people do talk this way…with just a few words. A line later comes this:

> Someone rattles the door knob. Mama calls, "Dale, you in there?"

This time, Dale's mother drops the verb of the sentence. "Dale (are) you in the there?" Once again the sentence becomes livelier without the verb in it.

Talking at Cross-Purposes

A second way of creating lively dialogue is for the people in the scene to talk to each other without entirely hearing or responding to what the other person is saying. This is called **talking at cross-purposes.** (This happens very frequently in life, so it is a good exercise to go to a restaurant and listen in on other's conversations to get examples of lively dialog.) Here is another line from the opening of Dale's story:

> I pick up the towel stuffed in the crack at the bottom of the door, spray air freshener all around, and unlock the door.
> Mama rushes in. She comes out with a sniff. "Thought you quit."
> "Yeah, going to college."
> "Not what I meant. You got a good job at Boeing."

In this exchange, Mama nails Dale for smoking in the bathroom. He pretends she is talking about quitting school, deflecting her criticism of him and the smell of cigarette smoke onto a subject of greater importance. She immediately picks up on the new theme—going to college—and tries to argue with him in the sentence, "Not what I meant." In this sentence, the subject and verb have again been dropped ("[That is] not what I meant").

Interesting, huh? Well, this is how people do talk to each other—ideas move quickly from one person to the next without either speaker finishing thoughts or sentences, especially when one person tries to convince another to change his behavior, opinions, or both.

If a writer has characters speak expressively about themselves without talking directly about the thing that matters most to them, this type of dialog is called "off the money." Alternatively, dialogue that says exactly what the character is thinking or feeling is often boring and lacks believability. This style of dialogue is called "on-the-money" writing. It takes a great deal of effort to become skilled at writing "off-the-money" dialogue, but the effort is always worth the trouble.

The Hook

A third approach to dialogue is to employ what might loosely be called a "hook." In this technique, one character says a line of dialogue, and then the character who speaks next repeats that line. For example:

> Janine shakes her head. "Tom, you're the most stubborn man I've ever met."
> Tom reacts with surprise. "Stubborn, me?"
> She laughs and hands him an apple. "Stubborn, me?" She shakes her head. "You seem so innocent."

In this brief exchange, the repetition of the lines of dialogue accomplishes several things. First of all, it is clear that Tom is really listening to Janine. Second, her line of dialogue nails a character quality in Tom that he has to deal with. Third, in handing him the apple, it clear that she likes Tom and may give him another chance to change, adjust, or do whatever he must to keep her interested.

As a writer, you may say, "Well, all of this is fine if you are a fiction writer, but I'm just writing life stories." In fact, all the techniques that I discuss are just as relevant to the palette of the nonfiction writer as to the fiction writer. If the life-story writer is skilled in the use of these techniques, he or she will begin to notice situations occurring in real life that reflect the techniques just discussed. So in the final analysis, the aim of these techniques is to help writers fine-tune their ability to listen to and observe life as it passes by.

— • • • —

Select one of your stories and look through it to see if your dialogue appears to be realistic and believable, yet fresh and lively. Allow different characters to speak in a different way. Experiment with dropping subjects and verbs, repeating lines of dialogue, and talking at cross-purposes:

Dropping subjects and verbs:

_____

_____

_____

Talking at cross-purposes:

_____

_____

_____

Repeating lines of dialogue:

_____

_____

_____

Inner Thoughts and Feelings

Writing inner thoughts and feelings is a huge challenge for any writer. When an author uses the third person (he, she, or they) to express a character and the character's actions, then the author may also use that third person to express intimate thoughts and feelings.

If an author chooses to write his central character in the first person, then other choices become available for expressing inner thoughts and feelings. Here is a moment from "The Garage" written by another student of mine, Karl Grey (the complete story can be found on page 122):

THE GARAGE *by Karl Grey*   (EXCERPT)

"Please let me in! Please unlock the door." I can hear my mother on the other side laughing at me. I'm pounding on the door, and I'm sure the whole neighborhood can see me in my underwear. They have all come out of their houses and are standing in the dark street watching me like I'm on the screen at a drive-in movie. I can hear them laughing at me and my mother laughing at me and I can't stand the way I feel. I am so filled with panic.

I pound and pound on the door, but all I hear is the echo of laughing from both sides colliding on me. It's like this dream that I have over and over. I am walking on a sidewalk when all of a sudden I'm naked. I want to hide so that the other people on the sidewalk don't see me so I duck around behind the row of trees that is between the street and the sidewalk but the street is full of cars and all of the drivers can see me so I go back around the trees but then the sidewalk people can see me and pretty soon they have all stopped and all of the cars have stopped and they are all laughing and blowing the horns and saying, "Look at the naked fat kid. Does he even have a dick?" The sound gets louder and louder and I can't get away.

CRASH!

The kitchen door flies off the hinges and wood splinters as it hits the stove on the other side of the kitchen. I am in the house before the door hits the ground. My mother screams, and the scotch and water breaks on the floor. My stepfather has his belt undone by now and is pulling it through the loops of his pants.

I am running, into the den, into the cool . . . and my back stings, again and again, as I drop to the floor and roll myself into a ball and take it on my back. I'm safe now. I'm inside myself, and nobody can see me while he continues to hit me with the doubled-up belt.

"Thank you, ladies and gentlemen, it's been a really big shoooow tonight. Next week on this stage, Elvis Presley"... and the crowd screams and my back stings, but it's cool in here and nobody can see me.

By using the first person, the writer makes the sense of the character's pain all the more acute:

I am running, into the den, into the cool...and my back stings, again and again, as I drop to the floor and roll myself into a ball and take it on my back. I'm safe now. I'm inside myself, and nobody can see me while he continues to hit me with the doubled-up belt.

The reader feels the sting of the belt even as the character has withdrawn into a deep, remote place inside himself:

...roll myself into a ball...take it on my back...safe now. I'm inside myself...nobody can see me...he continues to hit me with the doubled-up belt.

— • • • —

Look over several of your stories to see if you can add inner thoughts and feelings to the central character's response to the situation in which he finds himself. Notice that inner thoughts and feelings are only possible from the point of view of the person through whose eyes we are seeing the action unfold — the narrator.

Note: If you hope to get a sense of the inner thoughts and feelings of other characters in the story, you have to focus on their actions, their dialogue, and their facial expressions, much as a filmmaker would do.

_____

_____

_____

_____

_____

_____

_____

(Continue on your own sheet of paper.)

chapter 21

Employing the Principles of Art

For a writer's work to make sense to his or her audience and for the audience to remember what the writer is talking about, the writer as artist has to employ the principles of art. They must compose a story as a musician or a painter uses "composition" to create the impact they desire. Composition, in this context, means manipulating the elements of an artist's craft by means of the principles of art.

These principles—**repetition, balance, symmetry, variety, contrast, tension,** and **release**—are used by all artists at all times.

The most memorable works are those that rise above the literal: What the story *seems to be* about may not be what the story *is* about. The apparent subject matter may be visible on the surface of the painting, symphony, film, or novel, but the techniques (elements) of the artist's craft in conjunction with the use of the principles of art create a different meaning. We call this *subtext*.

How do we go about employing the principles of art as we write? Primarily, we create a motif (pattern) in the beginning of the story, change and develop it in the middle section of the story, and make its meaning clear as we resolve the story.

Many of the techniques we have already explored become more and more useful as we continually apply these principles of art. For example, when we build character, we may find *contrasting* goals, needs, wants, and intentions in each character. In a dialogue between two characters, we may find that *repeated* lines give emphasis to what is going on between the characters.

We may also find that visual and aural motifs may change somewhat from one section of the story to another giving variety to this pattern, as for example in the film *The King's Speech,* where the stuttering that occurs in the beginning of the story gives way to "unstuttered" speech when the king allows himself to swear, and then again when he has to make a momentous speech.

———• • •———

Once again, look over the stories you have written and select one story to analyze. Look through the story for instances where you have employed repetition, balance, symmetry, variety, contrast, tension, and release in the story. Perhaps the story is weighted too heavily in one section or the other, throwing off the *balance* of the story. That weight may stem from too much narrative, or too much dialogue, or too much inner thoughts and feelings. Too much of any of those options may cause the work to "tip" in that direction.

The story's arc should have a consistent pattern of tension and release to it so look for that as well.

In the following exercise, describe your use of the principles of art throughout the story. When you have finished ask yourself if everything feels balanced, with all questions that the audience might ask fully answered.

_____

_____

_____

_____

_____

_____

_____

_____

_____

_____

_____

_____

_____

_____

_____

_____

(Continue on your own sheet of paper.)

chapter 22

Developing Subtext

One of the most difficult yet rewarding tasks which the writer of creative stories undertakes is creating subtext. What the story *seems* to be about may not be what the story really *is* about. We call this additional meaning **subtext.**

In a play or a motion picture screenplay, the *writer provides the text*; that is, the actions taken by the hero/heroine and minor characters as well as the dialogue.

How the dialogue is interpreted so that believable relationships occur is the objective of the director and actors.

In Dale Crum's "Smoke Rings" we see this subtext emerging, little by little (see the complete story on page 117). Here are the narrator's lines that give us a picture of what is going on:

> I can't leave my good friend, Vera, a divorcée who works in the blueprint room.... Nor Joanne, the Catholic girl I sometimes go out with. Joanne's parents don't like Protestants. I really like Betty and Rosemary from our church. Mama does, too.

From this we see that he likes girls, and dates quite a bit, which gives us a picture of what might go on in the course of this story: an older, experienced man alone with a "willing" girl in a car during a long trip.

> She beams, "Mom says I can ride down to L.A. with you."
>
> Whoa! Her mother is a straight-laced woman from a straight-laced church. Takes two days to get to L.A. Unless you want to switch drivers and speed nonstop on that narrow, winding Highway 99.
>
> Elsie stops in her driveway. Her Mom, Mary, rushes to the car. "Oh, Dale, I'm so glad you decided to go. I trust you with Elsie. I know you will have an enjoyable trip."
>
> I think most mothers want to marry off their daughters by the time they're twenty years old. Wait a minute. Something's going on here.

From what is said, it looks like Elsie wants to go on a trip with Dale, and her mother hopes they get involved so they will wind up married—none of which is to Dale's liking.

"Huh-oh," this time I say under my breath. Takes only a second for the picture to develop in my mind. Mary wants me to take her daughter alone to California. She knows Charlie will find out. Poof! There goes Charlie.

I leer like Groucho Marx, "Long drive with me."

Elsie stares at me for a long time, then takes a cigarette from my package. I hold my Zippo lighter up, and she moves to the flame like a moth to a backyard barbecue. She inhales a little bit, coughs, and waves the smoke away from her face.

Here it appears that Dale sees Willie as no threat, and he makes a "we might have a night in a motel together" kind of a face. She appears to be thinking it over. In taking a cigarette from his packet of cigarettes, Elsie appears to be signaling that she is ready for a new experience.

Soon they arrive at a motel along the way and prepare to spend the night:

The bored clerk looks up from her *True Romances* magazine. She spits out of the side of her mouth, "Six dollars."

"Give me two adjoining rooms."

Her eyes flicker. She looks out the door before she hands me the keys. She makes me feel weird. Why spend the extra six dollars?

I carry the bags and balance on the bricks while Elsie splashes down the middle of the muddy walkway. After I plop down her bag, I move to the door.

She gives me the same quizzical look I saw on the clerk's face.

Now the reader sees that Dale plans to play it safe—no sex with Elsie. He doesn't want to risk winding up with her, just what her mom hopes will happen. No, he's going to outsmart them both.

We reach Los Angeles late the next day. I park in back of the women's dorm, shake out the kinks, and open the trunk. I turn with Elsie's bag and bump into a guy. He hugs Elsie and asks her, "Drive nonstop from Seattle?"

"Nope. Will, this is Dale," she replies. "Stopped in southern Oregon."

He persists, "Side of the road?"

"Nope. Motel."

She swivels her body away. Willie's face turns color. He slobbers into his red bandana handkerchief. I steel myself for his next question. In the same room?

He makes choking noises. No words come out. They stand nose to nose. I set her bag down, back out of the lot, and light up a cigarette before he clobbers me.

Now the reader thinks that Dale feels pretty good about himself. He has outsmarted Elsie and her mom in their desire to lasso Dale into early marriage. And he has not done anything to make Willie mad at him. Good for Dale.

> Four days later, I sit near Elsie in the cafeteria. She waves her left hand at me. A large rock sparkles on her ring finger.
> She giggles, "Me and Willie."
> I give her a big epiphany smile of admiration. "Congratulations."
> She outsmarted both her mother and me. Made Willie jealous enough to pop the question. I feel relieved. For once I don't need another cigarette. Any more may drive me crazy, may drive me insane.

Now we realize that Elsie had a whole different take than Dale did about what was supposed to happen, and her take turned out to be the true take. Careful Dale, sure he had outsmarted another calculating woman, realizes he has been too careful: He could have had a good time with Elsie without any consequences because she had her own take on things: make Willie jealous and get the ring whether Mama liked it or not.

The **text** of this delightful story is: Despite his lusts, Dale avoids the snares of a calculating mother and a lustful, carefree daughter. That is, he may have lust in his heart but he is too careful, too smart to fall for this mother and daughter plan—to trap him into early marriage. The **subtext** is: Women have agendas of their own and no man is smart enough to figure out all the angles when a woman knows what she wants.

Dale uses the motif of the cigarette throughout the story to underscore its meaning. In the beginning, the cigarette makes him an alien, an unwanted person in his mother's home, something of a fallen angel. In the development section, Elsie takes the cigarette from Dale and coughs, a sign that she is still an angel but is willing to be initiated. Dale, however, is suspicious of her motives (and her mother's) so he does not seduce her, and feels elated that he did not. In the conclusion, we see that Elsie is no angel. She is a temptress. Whether or not Dale seduced her or she seduced him, she played the seduction card with her fiancée and got what she wanted—the ring. In this way, the repetition of the cigarette motif led us to believe Dale's version of what was going to happen would be the tune that would be played, but in fact, as it turned out, her version of what was happening, her tune, was the one that she wound up playing—"Here Comes the Bride."

If there turns out to be a difference between the meaning of the text and the meaning of the subtext, this is a good thing. The reader gets that "seeing around corners" and "seeing what is not obvious" is a rich part of the story.

— • • • —

Select one of your stories to evaluate. Summarize for yourself what the meaning of the story is, as you see it. Is the meaning different from that provided by the dialogue and actions of the story?

Meaning of the story according to the text: _____

_____

_____

Meaning according to the subtext: _____

_____

_____

What accounts for the difference between the two possibly different meanings?

_____

_____

_____

(Continue on your own sheet of paper.)

———•••———

Take a look at the dialogue in this story. Does the dialogue reflect exactly what is on the speaker's mind, or do the actions of that character belie what he says, which creates a subtext for the scene? If the dialogue expresses exactly what the speaker is thinking, it may not feel realistic. After all, in life, we sometimes don't say exactly what we mean, even to loved ones.

Convert lines that are "on the money" to lines in which a hidden meaning is present, which the other person listening and responding may or may not get.

_____

_____

_____

_____

_____

_____

(Continue on your own sheet of paper.)

chapter 23

Separating the Writer's Voice from That of the Central Character

This last new aspect of story telling perplexes writers more than does any other. Writers of life stories find it especially difficult to grasp. Fiction writers know that, in creating an interesting central character, they must also create an interesting context (circumstances, setting, obstacles, and minor characters) within which the central character functions. Without these elements, the story will have little appeal.

On the other hand, life-story writers often feel that, because they sketch things that have happened, all they must do is simply record accurately what took place in the past.

The appearance of this task as "simple recording" is an illusion. We all know that the human mind plays tricks on us all the time. If we have a brother or sister with whom we have grown up, that sibling will rarely recollect shared experiences the same way we remember them. Moreover, many forgotten experiences lie in our subconscious, waiting for us to appear ready to deal with them. When we are ready, they emerge.

Writers using their life experiences must create both an interesting central character and a context within which the character operates, just as fiction writers do. A central character has a series of concerns (problems) that he wants solved. In most stories, the character either fails or succeeds. On the other hand, the writer's concerns may be something quite different. The writer may very well be concerned with making a statement about the way the universe works and not so much about the success or failure of the central character.

Very often, to create an interesting character and context means that writers of life stories must look hard for certain characters—that is, minor characters—who cause the central character to act decisively, revealing themself more fully in the process.

In Dale's story "Smoke Rings" (see the complete story on page 117), Elsie is a fully realized character who has her own agenda in life and fools both Dale and her mother. Dale is forced to admit that, if he thought he was in charge of the situation, he was wrong. Young Elsie was in charge. The laugh was on Dale.

Karl Grey's story "The Garage" (see the complete story on page 122) gives us a picture of a kid who doesn't have much going for him, a situation made more difficult by an indifferent mother and a brutal step-father. An action or movement on Karl's part becomes an opportunity for the insensitive parent to retaliate. So what can Karl do? What will he do? Eventually, he finds a place deep inside himself where no one can reach him; no one can touch him. A place of dignity and safety. At this moment, we like Karl. In his own way, he has triumphed over oppression.

When we write life stories, we know the disposition of the central character—his wants, his needs, his goals, his hopes and dreams. As readers, we want to see that character struggle to achieve his or her goals, not wallow in despair.

Consequently, we must make the minor characters that appear in the story more vivid than we might remember them at first. This does not mean we falsify them. No, indeed, we do not. But we do have to take a close, hard look at them, and to get behind their wants and needs, just as we would do if we were writing fiction.

Often my students say, "Well, at the time, my character didn't know these things. Yes, I know them now." (For example, the many layers of abuse a woman may have endured.) But the fact is, someone in the picture did know about the abuse and probably said something, even though it was ignored. That person becomes a significant minor character. (So often in life guides exist who know what is good for us but, at the time, we didn't understand what the person was saying, or we chose to ignore what they might have been saying.) All these minor characters must have a voice when we write.

Or in other circumstances, a minor character may be the voice of convention wanting the central character to behave the way everyone else behaves. The central character can only define themself by heading off in their own direction. Thus in Dale's story, his mother disapproves of Dale's decisions—quitting his job, going to Los Angeles, bringing Elsie along, smoking cigarettes. Dale's independence can only occur if he goes against his mother's wishes for him to lead a conventional life. This arc of his progress is made more difficult for him because he does love and respect his mother. Once again, a minor character defines who or what the main character is.

Another interesting example is the television series *Two and a Half Men*, created by Chuck Lorre. The central character, as played by Charlie Sheen, is a good-natured, easy-going, self-centered but fairly worldly fellow who does practically nothing in life (writes jingles) but makes a good living, affording him every opportunity to indulge in his self-involved life. Having a leeching brother and an irrepressible nephew move in makes him both uncomfortable, and ripe for a little growth.

Is his hedonistic life what the writer/creator of the show is wanting us to embrace? No, of course not. All the minor characters—his live-in housekeeper, his brother, his fiancée, his therapist, his mother, his ex-sister in law, and her new husband—push, nudge, and cajol Charlie to make changes, some of which he tries to make. And they do it in a way this is a lot of fun to watch. The enjoyment of the show is in watching Charlie struggle to hang on to his easy, male-chauvinist life as others insist he change.

• • •

Select one of your stories to examine and analyze. Ask yourself the following questions:

What does the central character in this story want?

_____

_____

_____

Does this want (goal) change in the course of the story? If so, how?

_____

_____

_____

Is this change in what the character wants the meaning of the story?

_____

_____

_____

If so, what role do the minor characters, their wants and qualities, play in the way the major character finds what he wants?

_____

_____

_____

Does the writer's goal for the story differ from the major character's goal? If so, how is this difference reflected?

_____

_____

_____

(Continue on your own sheet of paper.)

Once you have done the above exercise, go ahead and explore some of the stories you have previously written to see how you might be able to discern a difference between what the major character wants and what the author wants.

NOTES

_____
_____
_____
_____
_____
_____
_____
_____
_____
_____
_____
_____
_____
_____
_____
_____
_____
_____
_____
_____
_____
_____
_____
_____

Family History and Explorations

chapter 24

Telling a Family or Family-History Story

Now it's time for you to do another kind of story, a story told to you by your grandma or grandpa, or the oldest relative you know. Before you start writing, ask them to tell you…

1. how your family got to where they live now

or

2. where they lived a long time ago

or

3. any other story they would like to tell about how your family came to this country or community

Types of Family Stories

Family stories can be written in a number of different ways. Here is one example of a family story:

GRANDMA'S STORY

My grandma is in the kitchen making tea. She is looking out the window. She looks sad.

"Why do you look so sad, Grandma?" I ask.

She turns and smiles. "Today, sixty years ago, I left my home in Russia."

I sit down at the table near the stove. It is warm there.

"I remember it as if it were yesterday." Grandma pours me some tea. "My husband, your grandfather, was a very handsome man. He was about twenty. I was about seventeen. We were very much in love. One day we got a letter. It said he would be drafted into the army of Czar Nicholas. He did not want to go."

Grandma pours herself some tea. Her eyes get very bright. She smiles. "So in the middle of the night, we pack up our things, put them on our wagon and set out for America…."

Here we have grandma's story, but we also have a good sense of the warm, easy relationship between grandma and the writer. As a result, we believe the story without difficulty.

Sometimes a family history story may be a parent retelling something they did as a child. Here is an example of that kind of story.

LUPE ACOSTA'S STORY

I am sitting in the living room. My mom is watching a soap opera. She's kind of upset with me because my sisters and I have just finished getting into a fight. A commercial has just started. She looks at me and giggles.

"I remember when I was about eight years old, your grandparents left for the grocery store and left your aunt in charge of us. Me and your uncle Lobo got into a fight and he was chasing me all over the house. I hit him so he started crying. He left the room so that he could go and get a broom. He comes in yelling, 'Watch out Lupe. You're gonna get it.'"

I started laughing because I can just imagine my mom's and uncle's faces.

"Your uncle came charging at me full speed," she goes on. "I was standing by a big empty fish tank that your grandma had a long time ago. I moved and he ran into it but the broomstick broke it. When your grandparents got home, they asked, 'What happened?' I just looked at them and started laughing. Your uncle started crying and crying. Your aunt told them everything that happened so we both got into trouble."

I am laughing even more. Then she tells me, "You and your sisters are just like me and your aunts and uncles when we were young. We always gave your grandparents hell with all the fighting we did."

Lupe said she wrote the story because it gave her a different picture of her mother. As a playful child, her mother could appreciate what it was like to be a child. She wasn't always telling Lupe what she was doing wrong.

• • •

Go ahead and write your family story now. Use all the things you have learned. Include feelings. If it seems like a good idea to add dialogue, do so.

Use the present tense to describe what you and your relative
are doing in the present, ie. when the story begins. Use the
past tense to describe the story your relative tells.

_____

_____

_____

(Continue on your own sheet of paper.)

More Authentic Family Stories

Many of us who set out to write life stories are primarily interested in writing about the struggles and history of our parents and grandparents. Typically this kind of story is a simple narrative retelling of the past.

> My grandfather was born in the Ukraine. When he was 16 he was forced to serve in the Czar's army. After a year he escaped and made his way to America.

While reading this sort of narrative, we, the readers, find ourselves asking a number of questions:

1. How did the narrator hear his grandfather's story?
2. Who told him the story?
3. How do we know it is true?
4. How did the people involved (Grandpa and the narrator) feel about these events?

Out of a need to answer these questions, another, more authentic, way of telling family histories has emerged, one in which the feelings of both the storyteller and the writer are evident while the story is unfolding.

When writing this kind of family history, let the reader know how you learned about the story. Were you sitting on Grandma's knee or taking a walk with Grandpa? Let the reader know what you remember Grandpa or Grandma doing or feeling while they were telling you the story. That way we get both the story and your relationship to the storyteller. We will believe it and feel it more fully.

John Strong's "How I Became a Rebel" is a good example of this kind of writing.

- -

 (Note: In this story, the narrator, the teller of the story, happens to be the writer, John Strong, and then the reader experiences a story-within-a-story. This kind of story—a touching, personal experience with a famous or important person in history—might well be passed down within a family from one generation to the next.)

- -

HOW I BECAME A REBEL   *by John Strong*

I am nine years old and in elementary school in Clymer, Pennsylvania. The year is 1922. One day the teacher tells us, "Class, we have a special treat today. We have two visitors . . . who fought in the War between the States. They are here to tell you about it."

A few moments later they walk in. Two of them. They are old. With beards. Today is Veteran's Day, so they wear their uniforms, blue tunics with blue pants. One has the bars of a lieutenant on his shoulders. They walk slowly and sit down.

I am eager to talk to them. On both my father's and mother's side of the family, I have relatives who fought in the Grand Army of the Republic, the Union Army.

At the first chance I get, I raise my hand. "Sir," I say, "could you tell us about being in the war. What it was like?"

The old man's eyes come alive. "I suppose you want me to tell you about the bloody battles, don't you?" I nod. He shakes his head. "I won't do that. War is hell. Absolute hell. But I will tell you a story about the war," he continues. He leans back in his chair. His eyes get a faraway look.

"The war was over. The bloodiest damn thing you ever saw. My best friend Joshua and I decided we wanted to go to college together. We were lieutenants in the GAR, the Union Army, and we wanted to stick together. So we chose Washington and Lee University."

The old man smiled down at me. His eyes were soft.

"We enrolled in classes there. General Lee — Robert E. Lee, the commanding general of all the Confederate forces — was the president of the university, but we didn't see him much. Occasionally a parade in the mornings. But he marched out of step, on purpose, to make himself ordinary, nothing special. But we admired him nonetheless.

"Almost all the other men there had fought for the South. After all, General Lee had been their commander. They'd've followed him anywhere.

"One day we got a note from the office of the president of the college asking us to stop by. When we arrived, the general was waiting for us. He was a soft-spoken man. A little shy. But powerful. I almost saluted him. He came right to the point.

"'Gentlemen, I suppose it has not escaped your attention that most of the boys at this here school were once under my command in the late war.'

"'Yes, sir,' I said, eager to say something.

"'Well, then, since you are the only two fellows from the Union Army enrolled down here, officers too, I wonder if you might tell me . . . why? Why did you come here?'

"I looked at my friend, and he looked at me. Finally I spoke up. 'General, sir, my buddy and me, we figured that you were the best general of any of 'em, North or South. Wherever you went, that was the place for us.'

The old soldier stops for a moment. He takes a glass of water and drinks. Finally he goes on.

"The general stood and looked at us, then nodded. There was a faint smile on his face. He shook hands with us both. We left."

The classroom is as quiet as an empty church. The old soldier looks around the room at each one of us. "Think about that, boys."

— • • • —

Notice that in the story John speaks in the present tense, as if Clymer, 1924, were the present; but when the old soldier recollects the past, he speaks in the past tense. This is because the old soldier's recollection of 1865 was the past, even in 1924.

John's soldier speaks directly to us as well as to him. The result is that we experience the story through John's eyes. It is important for us as readers or listeners to know through whose eyes we are experiencing events at every turn in the story. It creates belief in the story. It also increases our interest because writer and teller have a relationship to share with us, in addition to the subject matter of the story itself.

A hundred years ago we would not have thought to ask, "From whose point of view are we seeing the story and is it to be believed?" Until the middle of the nineteenth century writers like Poe, Dana, Scott, Thackeray, Hardy, Melville, and many others told their stories from a godlike, omniscient narrative point of view, and readers accepted this point of view as believable. But in the writings of Stephen Crane, Henry James, and James Joyce, and in the dramas of Pirandello, readers became more aware of the person through whose eyes the story was being experienced and seen and of the subjectivity of the telling of one story.

For example, if we read a story told from the point of view of one sister who is obviously jealous of another, we know we are getting, in the telling of the story, other bias, other feelings, not the whole truth.

So, as contemporary readers, we no longer take for granted the truth of a story unless we know something about who is telling it. By recording the relationship of the storyteller to the writer of the story, we get a more authentic and believable view of the family history that is being told.

 In this kind of story, you as a child want to be in the story as your relative tells you the story. As the narrator, interrupt your relative from time to time and ask questions, just as John did in his story.

— • • • —

TITLE: A STORY FROM MY FAMILY HISTORY

_____

_____

_____

_____

_____

_____

_____

_____

_____

_____

_____

_____

_____

_____

_____

_____

_____

_____

_____

(Continue on your own sheet of paper.)

> To ask the author questions about
> "Telling a Family or Family-History Story"
> or to share your own thoughts,
> you can join the ongoing conversation at
> facebook.com/WritingFromWithin.

chapter 25

Researching a Family History

The explosive use of the Internet has opened up the possibility of bringing our pasts into clearer focus. Outfits such as Ancestry.com have compiled and computerized a vast amount of information so that each of us can now know who our forebearers were without expending a huge amount of effort.

For example, recently, Bill, a distant relative, sent a photograph of his snow-covered home in Virginia around the Internet to members of the family. I recognized his name and recalled to him a family story in which one of my students had known Bill's mother some sixty years before. My student's mother had helped Bill's mother and grandfather, Karl Kawakami, buy a house in San Francisco in the early years of the twentieth century, when owning property was exceedingly difficult for Asian families. Bill wrote back saying that memory had been a favorite of his mother, whose father was a well-known Japanese newspaper reporter in the early years of the twentieth century.

Bill and I began corresponding about our family: His great grandmother was a sister to my great grandmother. He had been researching his family for some time, the Clark family. Soon my former wife, Gail, became interested in this research, along with my first cousin Mary Ellen. Before long, we found a relative who had been a captain in the Union Army during the American Civil War: Bela Tecumseh Clark. Bela's middle name intrigued us because General of the Army, William T. Sherman, had a middle name — Tecumseh. What the link was we do not know, but some day I'm sure we will know.

A little more research informed us that Bela's father-in-law was one Colonel Sylvanus Thayer. On the official website of the U.S. Military Academy, Sylvanus Thayer is acknowledged as the "father of the U.S. Military Academy." Well, that surprised, even astonished, us — to think that such an illustrious person lay at the corner of our family history without our knowing about him.

A bit more research told us that he was an unmarried man. Thus we were on the wrong track. Well, perhaps not. Since there were two men of approximately the same age (one born in 1798; the other in 1785), both born in New England (Vermont and Massachusetts), we suspected a common ancestor, not too far back. As of this time we are researching that common ancestor…and have found half a dozen Thayers who also fought in the Civil War, most from Illinois and Michigan. More recently I found out from Bill that my great grandfather, Anson Culver, was a drummer boy in the Union Army.

Now the reason that I bring this up in a book about writing is that ultimately writing is about communication. Usually writing is about communication that moves from the writer to the reader. Lately, however, with blogs, websites, dot-coms and the like, communication is moving back and forth, more often than not.

Similarly, in a little project like this, a number of members of the family—Bill, cousin Mary Ellen, former wife Gail, and myself, Bernard, have all gotten to know each other a little better. Sister Mary Lee and cousin Tom have reappeared also. From a few facts, we have been able to piece together interesting fragments of life as the country moved from the eastern seaboard westward through the Ohio Valley and into the mid-west, Illinois and Michigan. We have shared family photos and memorabilia, and their significance, debated and analyzed.

In several instances the possessor of such memorabilia didn't quite know the significance, but other members of "the team" were able to identify who the subjects were in old photos. In fact, this group—Gail, Bill, and Mary Ellen—have given themselves a name: CHART—Clark Heritage Ancestry Research Team. (Hey, what am I? Chopped liver?)

These on-going tasks—identifying photos, noting the signatures of guests at weddings, finding links between generations, preserving stories—creates a wonderful bond among family members, as well as surprising links with "outsiders" such as my student Matt and Bill's mother, Yuri. My sons, Jeff—an airline pilot—and Will—a Marine who served in Desert Storm and Operation Iraqi Freedom—are both quite fascinated by our link to the father of the U.S. Military Academy.

Through blogs and dot-coms such as Ancestry.com, more and more families will find common ancestors, stories, photos, and the like, creating ever stronger family bonds. The history of every person's family is a history in miniature of the larger events that have taken place over centuries since the founding of our republic. In our case, it appears that our fore-bearers counted John and Pricilla Alden—among the first families of the original Plymouth Settlement in Massachusetts—as members of our family tree.

In this we are not unique, as many hundreds of families can easily trace their roots back to just such ancestors. Researching these roots is a fascinating task and has many, many benefits for those who undertake such efforts.

• • •

Using the Internet to begin your search and supplementing your search by using ancestry research websites, find out what you can about your mother's family as well as your father's family.

Begin with the first and last names of your parents then trace the family names back through your four grandparents and your eight great grandparents.

Parent—father: name and birthplace:

_____

Father's mother's name and birthplace:

_____

Father's father's name and birthplace:

_____

Father's grandfather's name and birthplace (father's side):

_____

Father's grandfather's name and birthplace (mother's side):

_____

Parent—mother: name and birthplace:

_____

Mother's mother's name and birthplace:

_____

Mother's father's name and birthplace:

_____

Mother's grandfather's name and birthplace (father's side):

_____

Mother's grandfather's name and birthplace (mother's side):

_____

— • • • —

When you have gathered as much information about your parents, grandparents, and great grandparents as you can, contact uncles and aunts, as well as brothers and sisters of your parents and grandparents to see if they have stories or more information about the relatives listed above. You may be surprised at how much information and memorabilia exists in attics, old trunks, garages, safety deposit boxes, and the like.

(In my case, I contacted a distant cousin on my mother's side who had pictures of our great grandfather who was a captain an Illinois regiment during the American Civil War…and still had our great grandfather's sword.)

Information obtained from relative (specify): _____

_____

_____

_____

_____

_____

_____

_____

Information obtained from relative (specify): _____

_____

_____

_____

_____

_____

_____

Information obtained from relative (specify): _____

_____

_____

_____

_____

_____

(Continue on your own sheet of paper.)

NOTES

Turning Stories into Fiction Writing

chapter 26

Writing Creative Stories

Writing life stories is to a writer as sketching is to an artist. It is a first step to creating something bigger. Leonardo da Vinci filled up many, many sketchbooks with ideas before he painted *The Last Supper*.

Doing sketches based on your life stories will help you do other kinds of creative writing, nonfiction and fiction. One kind of writing is called creating personal myths.

Myths & Fables

In this kind of writing, you find a legend, folktale, myth or fable that happened many, many years ago. You look for the meaning behind that myth or legend. Then you find a moment in your own life that illustrates that meaning or message. If you cannot find it in your own life, then you make up or imagine what is necessary.

Here are some examples:

THE TORTOISE AND THE HARE
(THE TURTLE AND THE RABBIT)

The tortoise and the hare started a race. The hare raced off to a big lead. The tortoise crawled along very slowly. Soon the hare got tired and rested. The tortoise kept crawling along. The hare saw the tortoise coming and bounded off. Soon the hare became tired again. The tortoise kept crawling. This time the tortoise crawled past the hare. The hare laughed, sprang to his feet and raced past the tortoise. Again he got tired, rested and let the tortoise pass him. When at last he started hopping toward the finish line, it was too late. The tortoise had passed the finish line.

Meaning or message: The slow but sure way wins out against the fast and furious.

PERSONAL MYTH OR LEGEND

Hector and Jorge are in love with Elena who likes them both but is not sure whom she wants to marry. Both men decide they will go to the United States to become successful.

Hector is a handsome young singer and trumpet player. He is a big success playing in a band. He makes good money, dates beautiful women and sends Elena expensive presents.

Jorge works as a box boy, learns English, becomes a citizen and works his way up to manager of the store. Every week he sends Elena a letter and a rose.

Sometimes Hector doesn't get work so he doesn't write to Elena. Sometimes she doesn't hear from him for several months. Then she gets an expensive present. But she gets a letter from Jorge every week.

In the end they each propose marriage to Elena.

Whom does she marry? Well, according to the legend of the tortoise and the hare, she marries Jorge. What would you do?

_____

_____

_____

_____

(Continue on your own sheet of paper.)

Look up the following myths:

1. the myth of Daedalus and Icarus

2. the myth of Sisyphus

3. the myth of Oedipus

4. the myth of Orpheus and Eurydice

5. another myth you know about, not necessarily of Greek origin

Summarize one of these myths:

_____

_____

_____

_____

What is the meaning or the message of the myth?

_____

_____

_____

_____

Now make up a personal myth from your life or imagination, based on the Greek myth:

_____

_____

_____

_____

Now that you have a story, what can you add to it that will make it better, based on your life-story writing skills?

1. present tense

2. feelings

3. dialogue

4. inner thoughts and feelings

Rewrite your story using or adding the present tense, feelings, dialogue, inner thoughts and feelings, and a thumbnail sketch of the characters.

Title:_____

_____

_____

_____

_____

(Continue on your own sheet of paper.)

Cross-Cultural Myths

The myths from ancient Greece continue to be of interest because they tell us so much about ourselves. They have formed a backbone for education in the Western world for the past 2,000 years.

During recent decades, a growing recognition of the great value of other cultures, particularly Latino, Black and Native American cultures in the United States, has awakened interest in their myths, legends, folk tales, and fables.

The following are examples of myths from diverse cultures:

1. The Coyote (The Trickster)—Native American
   Just when you have what you want, the coyote comes along and steals it away.

2. The Phoenix—Egyptian
   The Phoenix is a bird that lived 500 years then made a pile of spices in the Arabian desert, burned itself to ashes, and came forth from the ashes, to repeat the cycle.

3. The Hare—African

   The hare tricked all its victims into doing its bidding. When the people of the village set a trap for it, the village chief was the one trapped and the hare got away.

4. El Dorado—Spanish

   El Dorado was a mythical city located in the desert of the western United States where everything was golden.

5. Fountain of Youth—Spanish

   The Fountain of Youth was a spring filled with a liquid that enabled the user to remain young forever. People exhausted themselves in pursuit of this mythical spring.

6. Faust—German

   Faust was a man who made a pact with the devil. Satan granted him one wish, to have greater knowledge than anyone else. Then the devil forced him to pay the price.

EXERCISE

Drawing on your own particular cultural background, choose a myth, legend, or fairy tale told to you in your family, church, or school.

First tell the story of the myth:

_____

_____

_____

_____

_____

(Continue on your own sheet of paper.)

Now can you convert your family's myth into a story from your life or your imagination? If so, do it now.

Title:_____

_____

_____

_____

_____

(Continue on your own sheet of paper.)

Expanding Your Creative Vision

The following is another example of a highly creative story. After writing a few life stories to acquire the skills of using narrative, dialogue and inner thoughts and feelings, the writer created a series of stories about mammals and wrote each story from the point of view of the baby coming into the world, growing up and learning to fend for itself.

MOLLOKO, THE CALIFORNIA CONDOR   *by Inés Horovitz*

I can hear the wind blowing through the pine trees. It's sunny outside, and I am waiting for my mom or my dad to bring me some food. I live in a cave high up on a cliff. It's a little scary: I almost fell off a few times. I am also a little scared that a golden eagle will find me. My mom told me to watch out for them. I think I can hear my mom or my dad now: There's a hissing sound.

"Hi Molloko, good morning!"

"Hi Mom! I love it when I hear the hissing sound because I know you or Dad is near. How do you make it?"

"It's the wind going through our wing feathers."

I'm really hungry, so I'm very excited to see her! She smells really clean. I can tell she took a bath. I would love to take baths too, but I have to learn to fly first to get to a bathing place.

I flap my wings as hard as I can to let my mom know I can't wait for my food anymore. She stands beside me and opens her bill over my head, so I stick my head in it. Some food comes out of her throat. It's been in her tummy and it's a little digested already. I take the food in my mouth. After I swallow it, more food keeps coming. When we're done, I try to get my head out of her throat but I'm stuck. My mom puts her foot on my neck and pushes me down to the floor of our cave so my head comes out. What a relief! I can breathe now!

"What food was that, Mom?"

"It was a dead weasel I found on a big boulder. It probably fell off the cliff above."

"Have you ever caught any animals, Mom?"

"No, dear. We don't catch animals. We just find dead ones."

"But I like to play I catch things, Mom. I will catch animals when I grow up."

"You like to play that way because a long, long time ago, our great, great, many times great grandparents were different from us, and they hunted for their food. But we condors and vultures have changed over millions of years to just eat carcasses, dear. Our babies still play that way because you are born with the need to learn that skill, but you will lose the need to use it when you grow up. It's okay to play that way, though—it's fun, isn't it?"

A few weeks later I start walking out of our cave onto a narrow ledge, and I wait for my parents from there. I am a little afraid of flying still, but I have been flapping my wings inside our cave to practice and get stronger. If I fell off the ledge, I think I would be okay: I could flap my wings hard enough that I would not hit the rocks below too hard, I hope.

"Have you preened your feathers this morning?"

"Yes, Mama."

"They look shiny! I can tell you've been taking good care of them. Just a few spots need a little preening. I'll feed you, and I'll preen those spots after," says my mom.

I love it when she does that. I feel a little ticklish. Sometimes I preen her feathers, too.

"Molloko, you should start flying off into the canyon. We've had five full moons since you hatched. You are old enough now, and your feathers look great! You should start using them! I'm off to find more food now. See you later!"

I am feeling good now that my mom fed me. They don't feed me that often anymore: Some days they don't feed me at all. I can see some birds flying by from my ledge. It looks like so much fun! Maybe I could try flying off. Maybe I am ready to do it now. My heart is beating so fast, it feels like it's going to take off before I do. Here I go.... One, two, three! Weeeeeee!!!!!!

I'm off, and I flap my wings as hard as I can. They sound loud! At first I am going straight down, but then I manage to fly forward for a short stretch, and then my wings get tired and I start going down again. Mom, Dad!!! Anyone around???? Help!!!! There's a tree coming straight at me!!! "No, no tree, out of my way, move, move!" But it won't move. I crash right into it. OUCH!!!!!

I hold on to a branch for a while until I recover from my emergency landing. I'd love to get back to my nest! But I'll have to do it little by little. I'll try to get to a nearby sequoia tree as my first stop. It's not far. Maybe I can do it! I take off and lose height at first but manage to fly up a little and ahead!

"Here I come, sequoia! Stick out a branch for me!!!!"

But the sequoia won't listen. It just stays still, and I have to find a branch myself. It's hard, though! I can't really aim at anything to land on, I can't fly that well yet. I finally crash against a branch. OUCH!!!!

A few days later I make it back to the nest. I still have a hard time flying and aiming at a spot to land on, though. After a few days I start practicing again.

I am finally ready to go looking for food with my parents. We fly so high everything below looks tiny, even tinier than from the entrance to our cave. They show me some other caves and places where I could make my nest some day.

"Did other condors live in those caves before?" I ask.

"Yes. My great grandmother told me there used to be a lot of condors around here. But when people started finding these gold little stones in rivers around here they went crazy and started coming by the thousands. And it was very hard for us to find much food. And they soon started destroying the river banks looking for more."

"Are they still looking for those shiny stones, Mama?"

"Not much at all anymore. But it was too late when they stopped. Lots of people stayed to live around here. Over the years there were very few of us alive and when there was just one of us left, my grandmother, they took her to a place they call a zoo in a big city."

"What for, Mama?"

"They had her have babies with other condors from other zoos. When those babies grew they put them back in the wild. And here we are, living the best we can. When she was at the zoo, my grandma heard that now they are looking for those shiny rocks somewhere else, in the Andes mountains, where other condors live. They destroy the land to find those shiny stones. They go "BOOOOM!" and all the rocks fly. And they find their rocks and move on, looking for more."

"Can we go see, Mom?"

"No dear, it's too far. We don't fly that far."

"I hope they stop doing that, Mom!"

"Yes, someday the people who live there will realize it has to stop, the same they realized around here."

Note: Inés Horowitz, PhD, the woman who wrote this story, is a professor of paleontology at UCLA and the mother of a six-year-old girl. Ines wrote this story and several more like it, to convey her love of mammals—her specialty—to children.

— • • • —

Using narrative, dialogue, and inner thoughts and feelings, go ahead and write a creative story of your choosing. One fun exercise is to have small children or grandchildren you know illustrate the story as they envision it in their own minds. You can write a story from any number of interesting perspectives. For example, write a story from the point of view of an animal. Or an object, like a tree or a pencil. For another example of this type of story, see "Blackcat–Whitecat" on page 125.

> From time to time we will be adding new creative stories to the
> Facebook discussion site. For more of these stories see
> www.WritingFromWithin-Stories.com.
> To ask the author questions about "Writing Creative Stories" or
> to share your own thoughts, you can join the ongoing conversation
> at facebook.com/WritingFromWithin.

chapter 27

Further Developing Fiction-Writing Skills

Every writer—whether novelist, short story writer, playwright or screenwriter—has three basic tools with which to work: *narrative, dialogue,* and *inner thoughts and feelings.*

The novelist or short-story writer must be skilled at narrative and good at dialogue, and both have the advantage of being able to express inner thoughts and feelings directly.

The playwright has basically just dialogue and inner thoughts and feelings to work with. The action has to be simple and suggestive rather than literal. Inner thoughts and feelings can be expressed directly within each character who appears on stage.

The screenwriter must be skilled at creating narrative that can be communicated primarily through visual action and dialogue. His success, however, will derive from the way that he handles inner thoughts and feelings that can seldom be expressed directly.

The following is a suggested process for developing skills as a fiction writer:

1. Write a number of stories from your life experience following the steps described earlier in this workbook.

2. Move slowly and carefully through the basic steps and then through the advanced steps.

3. Take one of your life stories and convert it into a play and then a novel, or parts of a novel or a short story.

4. Find a story, incident or develop an idea that floats around in your head and allow it to come out as a novel, play, or screenplay.

5. Follow the steps advised in the Advanced Steps (see Unit II, starting on page 39).

6. If you are interested in writing plays or screenplays, join a local theatre group and write for the actors in the company. Pretty soon you will learn what you need to do to make actors comfortable with your work.

Tips on Writing Fiction

While play writing and screenwriting require specific techniques and further study than the tips provided in this book, most of the skills learned in life-story writing translate directly into the fiction medium, such as the way we uncover character by stressing the very real difference between the narrator's concerns and the character's concerns. Another crossover skill is using action to portray character. These techniques, when practiced in the writing of our own life experiences, will help us write more-authentic, more-believable (and more-salable) fiction. At the very least, the sketches we create when writing life stories enable us to draw accurately from life.

1. Whatever moment inspires you to write, go ahead and write it down. Do not worry about any of the techniques described earlier. Just get a hold of the vivid moment that comes up in your brain, then tuck it away and begin to develop a story around it. If your energy flags, just go to this moment for inspiration. Having done this has allowed me to write several novels of the Renaissance in Italy. Whenever my energy or resolve flagged, I went back to the scene I wrote many years ago that inspired me to begin this saga.

2. When writing a play, find the passion you have for the character(s) and go from there. You may dislike the character or not, as long as you have passion and the character knows what they want. Years ago I wrote a short scene about two alcoholics, one recovered and now a successful head hunter who has just had a hiring for a big entertainment company. Her boyfriend, a big, strong fellow who worked the pipelines in Alaska, never recovered and wants to head back to Alaska. The woman whose portrait in real life I drew upon was not someone I liked, but on stage she had such a clear sense of what she wanted (to seduce her boyfriend before he departed) that the scene was very successful and she became suddenly very attractive because of her determination to stop at nothing to seduce him one last time.

3. When writing screenplays, be sure that the format is correct from the beginning. The scenes must be written in Courier type, in a 12-point font, and the scenes must be written as follows:

```
EXT—MONTANA RANCH—DUSK

A solitary ranch house with outbuildings sits on a
plain between mountain ranges, set against a deep-
blue sky. A lonely windmill rotates slowly.

EXT—RANCHHOUSE—NIGHT
```

This simple indication is important because each scene must be scheduled on a production manager's board. "Day" scenes of a similar nature will often be grouped together, and shot, out of sequence. The same holds true for "night" scenes.

The narrative line—that is, the action, needs to be simple and direct.

```
Jed Davis—lanky and ill-shaven, with a smoldering,
purposeful intensity about him, strides from the bunk
house to the main building.
```

Notice that he is described as "striding," not walking or ambling. Strong verbs are necessary, and unnecessary adjectives and adverbs must be left out.

```
A voice cries out in the darkness.

                    FEMALE VOICE (O.C.)
          Hold it right there, Mr. Davis

A shot rings out. A bullet pings off the ground near
his leg. Davis stands his ground.

                    JED DAVIS
                    (whining)
          Ain't be meanin' ya no harm, missy.
```

Here, his action is resolute (He stands his ground) but his words are servile (Ain't be meanin'...) so we don't trust him.

Generally, writers stay away from telling actors exactly how the character feels or acts (whining) but sometimes it helps—if action and dialogue work at cross-purposes—to give a little indication.

All the techniques we have discussed earlier in regards to character and dialogue can work in such scenes. The trick will be to tease from the scene what the inner thoughts and feelings of the characters are. In film this will result from the actions and dialogue of the characters.

4. When writing novels and/or short stories, practice getting behind each character in a scene so that we, the audience, understand what that character wants and what that character will do to get what they want.

One of the very best short stories ever written in this regard is Ernest Hemmingway's "The Short Happy Life of Francis Macomber." Macomber, a wealthy sportsman on safari in Africa with his wife, has just run from a charging lion when the story opens. His wife expresses her contempt for his cowardice in needling, insulting language and then by cuckolding him with the Australian guide that night. It appears that she will do almost anything to keep Macomber in his place, at her feet, and seems to have such a hold over him that she can do all this with impunity.

Oddly enough, Macomber is not especially put off by any of this, which results in a grudging respect from the guide. The following day, Macomber again puts himself in harm's way, this time with a charging water buffalo. Unlike the day before, he stands his ground and fires until the buffalo falls. At the moment the animal is struck, Mrs. Macomber fires her own rifle, splitting open her husband's skull.

Apparently, while Macomber was finding his manhood, Mrs. Macomber faced the prospect of a husband no longer willing to sit at her feet…and perhaps ready to rid himself of her…so she did away with him, a spider lady devouring her mate.

For more about this story and how it was made into a movie starring Joan Bennet and Gregory Peck (a very bad movie) and how the author rewrote the screenplay, please see *Writing from Deeper Within* (2013) and *Writing from Within: The Next Generation* (2013).

— • • • —

From the life stories you have written, select a story and convert it into a fictional short story by placing your most interesting character in a completely fictional situation and seeing how they react. If the story appears to be successful, continue to place fictional obstacles in front of the character and allow them to solve problems based on the character qualities they possess.

_____

_____

_____

_____

_____

(Continue on your own sheet of paper.)

— • • • —

When you have finished the above exercise, try converting your short story into a screenplay and then into a short play, being careful to observe the conventions that I mentioned in steps 2, 3, and 4.

_____

_____

_____

_____

_____

(Continue on your own sheet of paper.)

Now that you have completed these exercises, go ahead and dive into that great pool of creativity called novel/play/screenwriting…but don't quit that day job, not quite yet.

Final Thoughts

Writing creatively provides untold pleasures for those of us who have committed ourselves to it over a long period of time. Yes, it's very satisfying if people want to read what we have written. In fact, some of us are able to make a living at it. And if we are able to write what we want to write and make a living at it, then writing becomes the best of all possible worlds. Yet whether we make a living at writing or not, writing creatively has enormous rewards.

Why is that? First of all, doing something creative with one's life fills a huge need inside of us, a need that many recognize but do not know how to answer. Whether one paints, sculpts, plays jazz, or acts, that creative need is fulfilled.

Yet a special kind of satisfaction exists in being or becoming a *writer.* When we write creatively, we have the opportunity to create *a universe parallel to the world in which we live our lives.* In this universe, we create something out of nothing. Characters come to life because we set them in motion, against a backdrop of our making, overcoming obstacles that we thought up using our imaginations. This parallel universe may or may not touch the world in which we live.

In writing a novel or a play, we get to leap into that parallel universe and stay there for as long as the writing takes, and we can revisit that universe at any time. The particular joy for us as playwrights is that each new set of actors in our plays will provide a different sense of what that parallel universe looks like. As novelists, we get to use words to paint portraits that are exactly what we want them to look like. As screenwriters, the picture in our minds of what the parallel universe looks like may or may not be the parallel universe that the director sees and creates. But the joy for us all as writers is in creating parallel universes of fascinating characters, interesting stories, and character arcs, as well as symbols, that reach deep into the readers'/audiences' minds and hearts, enabling them to participate in the "ride" along with us.

The techniques, approaches, tips, notes, and asides that you, the reader, have worked with in this workbook have been given to you so that you, too, can create your own parallel universes.

In the course of our lives, as we grow and change, we will get certain things...and we will lose certain things that we thought were dear to us. But when we write, and create our own parallel universes, these universes come to exist apart from us. Once we have created them, they can never be taken away from us because, once created, they exist...in a world of their own.

Now, its time for you—the reader—to create your own parallel universe(s) and experience the joys of writing.

unit v

Stories

The following stories were written by members of my writing classes over a period of some thirty years. Most of the students were older adults, reflecting back on an earlier time of life. From time to time, a younger student would appear, a person like Liz Kelly who had just dropped out of high school and made her way to Los Angeles where she appeared one day, out of nowhere, fortunately for us. Other interesting stories may be found in my new books: *Writing from Deeper Within* and *Writing from Within: The Next Generation*. All these stories, and those from *Writing from Within: The Next Generation* and *Writing from Deeper Within*, are also available to read and download at www.WritingFrom Within-Stories.com..

— • • • —

Eddie White   *Eddie is 70 years old. He grew up in rural Louisiana in the 1920s. The family moved to Cleveland, Ohio, and eventually Los Angeles where Eddie worked at odd jobs, played the saxophone, and became friends with jazz musicians Buddy Collette, Eric Dolphy, Jackie Kelso, Chico Hamilton, and Charlie Mingus. He tried his hand at boxing but at 5'5" he had a short career. After thirty-six years working for the post office, Eddie retired and now writes much of the time. He wrote this memory of a time when he was seven years old.*

THE OVERHEAD BRIDGE   *by Eddie White, Age 70*

I love to walk to the post office and pick up our mail. The post office is about two miles from Granny's house in downtown Ruston, Louisiana. Our box number is Box 107. I remove the mailbox key from the string around my neck and open our mailbox.

"Ahh, Ooooweee!" I yell to myself. I count to myself. "Granny has a lot of mail today." Because my mother is a school teacher and helps me with all of my school work along with her two youngest sisters, Baby Lowell and Sally Brooks, I learned to read very good and I have a very good knowledge of words and a better-than-most-kids understanding of the language. With three good teachers any kid can learn fast, at least something. Since I was three years old, I read better than most kids. I am seven now.

"Oh! Here is a letter from my Mother Dear; wonder if she has any money in it for Granny and me? One is from Aunt Brooksie, another from Baby Lowell. I bet they want something. They are away at school, college or something!"

"Ooooo, here's one from Aunt Anna. She hasn't written in a long time; this one is from Aunt Tee. (Lucyellen). I don't know why we call her 'Aunt Tee.' And here is the last one — a letter from good old Uncle Charlie, Granny's oldest son." This should make my grandmother happy, six letters in all, but I know what she will say when I get home. "Sonny, we didn't get no mail from Little Brother." Everyone calls Uncle John Glover Harvey either Little Uncle or Little Brother or the Baby Boy. Lawd! Lawd! Why don't he ever write just to let me know how he is getting along. I keep so worried all of the time wondering if something has happened to him. My baby got his leg cut off riding them freight trains when he weren't but nine years old, and has been a-hoboin' ever since, just ridin' the rails all over this land. He's been in every state in the country I 'spect. Lawd! Lawd! Have mercy!"

It seems that Granny would know by now that Little Uncle only writes to her or anyone else when he needs some money or something. We see him once in a great while. One day Little Uncle will come home for a day or so, then he will leave just like he came, like Santa Claus. Only Little Uncle won't bring anything but himself. "I just cain't stand to hear a freight train whistle blow. I just have to put on my travelin' clothes and go." That's what Little Uncle tells everyone.

"Hey there, boy!" One of the mail clerks hollers at me as I am walking out the door of the Post Office, "Tell your grandma that sure was a good chocolate cake she mailed to her daughter. Be sure to tell her to make a bigger cake next time so everybody in our post office can get some." He laughs real loud. "Heh! Heh! Heh!" I turn and look back at him. He kind of throws back his head a little. He has a very red face, a big throat, and he is the one I have seen up close with the wrinkles in his neck like a turkey.

I say nothing as I wonder to myself, "Is he one of the kinds of people that the rich white people call 'cracker trash'?" I am getting close to the old overhead bridge. It is made and shaped like a big rainbow. I have to cross the bridge going to and from the post office. Trains going out of and coming into town pass under the overhead bridge.

Sittin' on an old cane-bottom chair at the bottom of the crossing of the bridge is a very old, gray head white man. He is talking to a very big white boy as he kind of rocks back and forth in his chair.

As I get near them I see that the boy is about Baby Lowell's age, around seventeen or so, and he is not old and ugly looking like the old man. The boy is bareheaded. His hair is short, light-colored, and sandy-looking. The old man has on a dirty pair of raggedy-looking overalls and an old straw hat that has a hole in it. Neither of them have any shoes on, just like me. Because both the old man and the boy are poor-looking, I think that they must be nice and not mean white people, like that old post office clerk who ate up Baby Lowell's chocolate cake that Granny had baked and mailed to her.

As I walk by the two, the old man and the boy, I kind of smile at them, thinking they are nice people.

"Wait a minute!" shouts the big boy real mean and ugly-like. "Whatchall en you hanes?" He drawls out nasty and slow.

"It's mail for my Granny," I whisper, kind of scared but not too much because the ugly old man is nearby.

"Gimme dat dare mail," he drawls, snatching the mail from my hand. I look kind of long at the ugly old man and wait for him to make the big boy give me back our mail. Being little and the boy being big, I know that the ugly old man will be on my side and will make the boy give me back my mail. The mean old gray-headed man just grins his toothless grin and watches me. Tobacco or snuff spit drools down the corner of his ugly mouth which seems to sit almost in the middle of an ugly, odd-shaped face. He has greenish birdlike eyes that shift from me to the big boy. He reminds me of a chicken hawk.

The big boy begins to open my mail. He takes his time and reads the letters very slow to the old man, and they laugh at anything they think is funny. Because Granny cannot read or write, all the family members know that I read her mail to her. They write large and clear, and are sure to use words I can understand.

The big boy stumbles across a word that he cannot pronounce. It is an easy word, at least for me. He begins to stumble and spell out the word. "Let me see," he stumbles, "Ppp-rrr-o-gram? Prigrin-UH! Wonder what the hell is that?"

"It's not prigrin. It's program. Don't you know what a program is?" I ask him.

"Listen heah! You shut up, nigger! Don't you every dare to make a fool out of a white man! Do ya heah me, nigger boy?"

"Yes!" I answer.

"Whatta you mean yes. Don't you know you be talkin' to a white man? Yo folks better teach you yo manners 'fo you grow up an gits lynched. We love ta have neck tie parties for you smart uppity niggers. They want ta teach you to grow up right and respect white folks! You heah me, boy?"

"Yes sir," I answer. Tears begin to run down my face to the hot ground. It is not the word nigger or saying yes sir that makes me cry. It's the reading of our mail — our mail — granny's mail.

He puts all of the mail in the right envelopes. I think he is trying to let me know that he can read as well as I can, but I know that he can't. He gives the mail back to me.

"Now you git! I wantcha ta git! Git ta runnin'! Don't ya dare look back!" He slaps his hands hard and loud, and kicks at me. I jump back. He misses. I run almost all the way home. I am mad and scared as I run home. Two miles is a long way for a seven-year-old, so I run some but trot most of the way. I think of the old man and the big boy. How they stink. I think it is a very hot day and both of them are mean and stinking. But "the ugly old man stinks worst than the boy," I say to myself. "Maybe it's because the old man has been meaner and stinking longer than the boy." There is a difference between the postal clerk and the mean two. The postal clerk must be what rich white people call "cracker trash," and the mean two must be what rich white people call "poor white trash."

Granny works for a real rich white lady sometimes, and Granny tells me that when Mrs. Satterfield leaves her home for any reason, she tells Granny, "Now Lucinda, effen any niggers at all come by heah a-beggin for food while I'm gone, I want you to be sure and feed the niggers, but effen any poor white trash come by heah for anything at all, I want you to call Sheriff Thigpen and get them the hell away from my premises. Don't give THE TRASH a damned thing! Let the trash starve to death! That's what they deserve. They been free all their born, no account days. Now do you heah me, Lucinda?"

"Yes'm, I heah you, Niss Satterfield."

One day I asked Granny, "What do you do when the beggars come by, Granny? Do you do what Mrs. Satterfield tells you to do?"

"God don't love ugly, chile. I just feeds them all who comes by begging for food. I feeds them all, black and white alike."

I am finally home. It seems like I have been gone all day. I hurry into the house. Granny can tell I have been crying, and I am a little out of breath. "Why what's the matter, chile? What's the matter? Tell your Granny."

I tell Granny all about it. The South bein' what it is, nothing can be done about what happened to me. Granny pulls me to her and whispers, "We will just have to take it to the Good Lord in prayer. He will wipe away all tears and he will wash away all sorrow. Let us try and forget about it. God changes things, Sonny."

I think to myself just before getting ready to go to bed, "Granny is right. Granny is always right. My Granny is always right? There are no tears, and no sorrow and no anger."

Now I look back and laugh at it all—but how can I forget?

— • • • —

Florence Mayweather   *Florence spent much of her life in the rural south where her father, mother, brothers, and sisters lived as sharecroppers for most of her young life. The family dreamed of one day leaving the farm, but sharecropping did not provide them a way out, at least not until this story took place. Eventually Florence found her way out and made it to Los Angeles.*

LEAVING THE PLANTATION   *by Florence Mayweather, Age 72*

"It's feeding time," I can hear my father yell after he comes home from working the fields. My younger brother and I tag along to help care for the animals. Milking cows, feeding chickens, and slopping hogs is just another job to be done as part of our daily farm life.

We grow ever so tired and weary of working the plantation from sun up to sun down. Oh, how we long for a better life. My father and brothers often complain of getting overheated in the corn crops, or having to plow the fields in the heat of the southern sun. Time and time again things become almost unbearable and my brothers talk of leaving the plantation, one by one. We can always make ourselves feel better by vowing to save enough money to buy our very own house.

Poor crops and the low price of cotton make this almost impossible, because all sharecroppers are paid at the end of each year.

For many years my father is given a drink of whiskey and a pat on the back and told, "Sorry, Henry, but you did not make it out of debt this year."

"Those words would always make my heart ache," my father says.

The land owner attempts to pacify him by saying, "Now, Henry, if you and your children work hard, I am sure you will make it out of debt by next year."

My father tries to explain to him the things that we need just to be able to exist.

"Don't worry about a thing," the land owner says to him. "Haven't I always taken care of you and your little colored children? I have made arrangements at the general store and you can get a few things that you need there."

My father says, "Yes sir, Mr. Temp."

Mr. Temp places a big cigar in his mouth, unscrews the cap on the whiskey bottle. "Have another drink, Henry," he says. "I look forward to drinking with you good colored folks at the end of the year."

Sometime during the early forties, just when we think our dreams are never going to become a reality, farmers all over the South have a good year, crops are excellent, the price of cotton goes extremely high. There has been some talk among the share-croppers that absolutely no one is going to be left in debt this year.

They are right. The land owner comes and pays my father more money than we have ever seen in our lifetime. We have more than enough to buy our own house in the little country town of Keo, Arkansas, located twenty-five miles away from our home, where we are sure to live a more progressive lifestyle.

Now that we have the money, I am waiting for my parents to say that we will soon be moving any day. We know that my father is a bit hesitant, but we do not know why.

Then one day without warning he comes home with a big car—long, black, shiny, and new.

He has a big smile on his face. When we see that big car we have smiles on our faces, too. My mother meets him at the door with no smile on her face.

"Henry, what is this?" my mother asks.

"Well, Florence, as you can see, it's a car," my father answers.

"What about our house?" she asks.

"We can get our house next year," my father replies.

Somehow my mother is able to contain her tears, but she is not able to maintain her sanity.

"I can't wait another year!" she shouts and glares at my father. "If it's left up to you we will never get off this plantation."

My mother starts running around kicking chairs and pounding on tables. Many angry words flow from her lips. By now any smiles that we have had on our faces about that car have faded. Spellbound, we sit, watch, and listen, as our mother verbally fights with our father over spending the money on a car that we were going to use for our house. She accuses him of being afraid to leave the plantation. She tells him that he had to have received encouragement from the overseer to do such a thing. My father has little to say in defense of himself. I don't think there's anything he can say.

When it is all over, my mother has succeeded in painting such a clear negative picture of my father even we can see it. She has made him look as if he has less than a bird's brain.

We sit without movement, looking at him with big sad, glassy eyes, feeling little or no sympathy for him. It is obvious whose side we are on.

The next few days at our house are sheer gloom. The gloom is lifted when my mother takes matters into her own hands and announces that along with the leftover money we are going to sell the animals to help make payment on our new house. My older sister and brothers are happy. My younger brother and I are oh, so sad, because we grew up with most of those animals that she is talking about selling and to release them isn't going to be easy.

These animals that are being sold are like members of our family. For example, Old Rose, our brown and white cow. She is gentle as a lamb. She had never kicked over a bucket of her milk in her life. Old Rose is first to go. Then there is Fat Sam, the hog. We had raised Fat Sam from a little pig. Sam is so greedy he used to slurp all the slop from the other hogs and squeal long and hard if we did not give him more. As much as we complain about him we cannot hide the pain when it is Fat Sam's turn to leave. Tears roll from my face as I say goodbye to most of the animals I have known as a child. I have these same uncontrollable tears when it is time to close the front door on the old plantation farm house that had been my birth place and the only home I have ever known.

———— • • • ————

Liz Kelly   *Liz Kelly was 17 when she wrote this story. Shortly after the incident described in this story, which occurred when Liz was sixteen, she dropped out of school, left Wyoming, and came to Southern California where she began working as a live-in housekeeper. On her one morning a week off, she would come to one of my life-story writing classes.*

TANK TOP   *by Liz Kelly, Age 17*

With my limited wardrobe, I don't know how I am ever going to dress cool. It's hard to get noticed being only a sophomore, and I don't want to dress like a geek. I stare into my closet; same old shirts, same old pants, same old skirts. I've worn every combination of clothing possible, and this morning I don't know what I'm going to put on.

I glance out the window. It's a dark gray morning blanketed in soft white snow. It looks so quiet and peaceful. I turn back into my room and cross over to my dresser. I open the middle drawer of the old antique and absentmindedly search through the muss of clothing for a possible outfit. An idea strikes me as my hand passes over a dark gray tank top. I reach back and grab the top from the pile.

"Okay, I'm on a roll now," I think to myself. I slip the top over my head and stride back over to my closet. I take the dark brown cords from their hanger along with the light purple oxford. I'm dressed within seconds, and I open my door and step into the hallway. I can smell the coffee and toast coming from the kitchen.

I hear the showers running, and I know that everyone is up. I look at myself in the full-length mirror that hangs on the rough wood wall. "Not bad. Definitely different, but not ugly," I think. I tuck in my shirt and unbutton the top buttons so that the gray tank shows. I go back in my room to find my old high tops. I want to look casual. I pull my laces tight and then go in search of breakfast.

In the kitchen I run into my older brother, Pat. He's a year older, and we don't get along all that great at times. "A bit revealing, isn't it?" he comments on my shirt.

"No. I'm not showing anything," I shoot back at him.

"Just a little cleavage." He turns back to pouring his milk on his cold cereal. I stand on the other side of the big counter and concentrate on making myself some toast.

"Good morning," says Dad as he comes in and pours himself a cup of coffee.

"Good morning," we respond simultaneously.

Dad looks at me. "Is that what you're wearing to school?"

"Yes," I say.

"She's setting a fashion statement," Pat chimes in.

"I wear it today, everyone else wears it tomorrow," I laugh.

"Go change," Dad says. Pat and I stop laughing. (Pat looks away. If he needs to stand up for himself he does, but otherwise he tries to steer clear of Dad.) I look at Dad's face, searching for a clue to what's going on. I'm not sure if he's really angry. His face is serious, and his brow is furrowed.

I don't wait to hear him yell at me so I take off to my bedroom to change. I hear his heavy footsteps in the hallway. I study the closed door of my room, the planks so carefully put together yet not even touching, the smooth black handle and the solid bar that latches the door shut.

The latch raises sharply, metal clanking on metal. The unforgiving wood creaks at me in warning. "Oh, God," I think. "Why did I have to dress this way? Why didn't I know better?" I watch, unmoving, as my father gives the door one hard push and it sails open, slams into the far wall, and slowly bounces back to its resting place, quivering violently all the while.

In three long strides my father is across the room, and he grabs me by the arms. I'm flung from the window to up against the bunk bed.

My head cracks soundly against the old wood frame of the upper bunk, but I dare not reach my hand up to try to soothe away the pain.

"You are not wearing that to school," he screams. "Don't you have any goddamn decent clothes?"

"No," I want to scream back. "I'm trying to make do with the little that I have," but I don't scream it. I know I have to take his shit. He points his finger at me. His hand is becoming worn with age, but I know how strong that hand still is. He jabs me forcefully in the chest.

"This is my house! I make the rules, and if you are going to live here then you better damn well follow them." His finger is the only thing that keeps his fist from hitting me again and again as if trying to stay in beat with my pounding heart.

"I won't cry," I tell myself. I bite my lip and hold back the tears. "I'll change my clothes, and I'll follow his rules, and I'll take his shit, but he is never ever going to see me cry because of him." I look him in the eye and listen to every word he says. I ignore the shaking of my legs and the tears welling up in the back of my eyes. He gives me one hard shove, and I sit down hard on the bottom bed.

"No daughter of mine is leaving this house dressed like a whore!" he says with finality and storms out of the room. I sit on the bed not daring to move, still shaking like a leaf.

"I am not crying," I say to myself over and over. "It's okay." I take a deep breath. "I'll leave. I'll go live with someone else. I'll run away. I will get out of here somehow, some way." I bring myself to my feet and walk to my closet. "He doesn't care. He never has and never will. Just wait 'til I'm gone."

I grab a different shirt from its hanger and change the shirt I have on. Then I take off my shoes and change my pants for jeans. Off in the distance I hear a door open and then slam shut again. "Good. He's gone to school," I think. I open my door and step into the hallway to check myself in the mirror. Pat comes from the kitchen and watches for a moment as I straighten myself in the mirror.

"The shirt really was revealing," he says.

"It was not that revealing," I argue.

"Liz, if I was Dad, I wouldn't let you dress like that either. You let your boobs hang out, and you'll have every redneck in the school staring at your chest," Pat tells me.

"I am not that big," I say.

"You have big boobs," he says and walks past me into the bedroom.

"Some free country we live in. I can't even dress the way I want to. I was hardly dressed like a whore. Dad can say what he wants and do what he likes, but as soon as I'm gone, I'm never speaking to that bastard again." I talk to myself tough, and I act tough, but my insides feel like spaghetti. I go back to the kitchen, acting as normal as I possibly can.

I eat my toast, trying to keep from choking. My younger brother, Michael, looks at me from across the table with his big brown eyes and just shakes his head. He's three years younger than I am but smart for his age. He believes in keeping his nose clean. He reads his books and does his homework.

I finish getting ready for school and step out the door into the icy cold morning. I slide my feet across the frosty porch and down the slippery wooden steps. Crunch, crunch, crunch. My footsteps are the only sounds in the snow. Thud, thud, thud. In my mind I hear his finger banging into my chest.

"Damn it. I am not going to cry. I have my pride and if I let this little incident get to me then I'm never going to survive the real world." The school isn't too much farther. The gray paved road stretches forever though, right up to the gray sky. When I reach the school door, I take a deep breath, trying to calm my shaken nerves.

"I pray to God I don't run into him," I tell myself. "It really sucks that my dad teaches at the high school, but I don't see him." I dump my stuff in my locker and go to join my friends in the hall hangout. I see my friends, Lori and Joszi.

"Hi, guys," I say.

"Hey Liz, how's it going?" they ask.

"Fine," I reply. Lori gives me a funny look. I'm trying as hard as I possibly can to hold back the tears that seem to be forming in my throat.

"Liz, what's wrong?" Lori asks.

"Nothing," I say as I turn and quickly walk away so they won't see me crying. I only take a few steps, then I dry my eyes and turn and walk back.

"Liz, there's something wrong," Lori says. She puts her arm around me and guides me into the counselor's office. Mr. Cothern, the counselor, gives me a knowing look. I've been here before. Lori sits me in a chair, and I put my face in my hands and cry.

Lori leaves to go to class, and Cothern and I go into discussion.

"I can't live with my father anymore," I tell Cothern. "I can't handle it."

Cothern gives me a serious look. Well, as serious as his looks ever get. Mr. Cothern is a tall man who reminds me of a character out of a cartoon strip. His eyes are always laughing, and I don't think he takes me seriously.

"Cothern, I'm serious," I try to convince him.

"Liz, your dad isn't going to move out, and if you stick around things are going to get better. You can work them out."

"Fine," I say.

I sit and listen a while longer, then I go back to class. I know, only too well, that things are not going to change.

P.S. I began to see that my father wouldn't change so I had to. I dropped out of school and moved to Los Angeles from Wyoming. On my day off, I took Mr. Selling's writing class. I sent my stories back to my family. They began talking about all the things that had happened in the family. My father's rage and the alcoholism that triggered it were part of the discussion. They've been getting help.

• • •

Dale Crum   *Dale grew up on a farm during the Great Depression, a hard time in Arkansas. Both his father and mother were solid, God-fearing people, although his teacher/father was a big fan of F.D.R. Tired of his small-town roots, Dale joined the navy just before WWII. After the navy, he followed his parents to Seattle where they had moved during the war. Dale got an education through the G.I. Bill and went to work for Boeing in Seattle. Later he met the woman of his dreams and they settled in Southern California.*

SMOKE RINGS   *by Dale Crum*

My cigarette smoke drifts towards Mama's open bathroom window. I smoke two packs of Camels a day and crave nicotine early. Sunshine splashes on the pink shower curtain. Multicolored gold fish fluoresce among its folds.

Reminds me of tame Calicos, orange Orandas, and Bubble Eyes in the Marshall Islands. They swam close to my navy face mask in the coral reefs only three years ago. Wish I were there, now. These rainy Seattle streets depress me.

I stand up and look in the mirror. Out-of-focus wallpaper surrounds bloodshot eyes and scruffy whiskers. Eeeyoo, my breath smells rotten. My tongue feels like sandpaper. I hate these cigarettes! Or, rather, I hate myself for liking them.

"Stunt your growth," my dad used to say.

But he said that about playing with myself, too.

Someone rattles the doorknob. Mama calls, "Dale, you in there?"

I yell, "Won't be long" and reach for the Listerine. Oh, didn't think she would get up before seven o'clock. Too cold to go outside and smoke. I pick up the towel stuffed in the crack at the bottom of the door, spray air freshener all around, and unlock the door.

Mama rushes in. She comes out with a sniff. "Thought you quit."

"Yeah, going to college."

"Not what I meant. You got a good job at Boeing."

"Just made up my mind. Talked to Elsie about it."

She frowns, "Oh, her? You like her?"

"She's a college sophomore in California. She'll show me around."

My B-50 flight control rigger's job only pays one dollar and ten cents an hour. That's union swing-shift wages, too. Boeing hired me a year ago for seventy-five cents an hour. Maybe Harry Truman here in the beginning of his first full term can kick start the peace-time economy.

I sold my 1941 Buick sedan for eleven hundred dollars. Bought a cream puff '37 Chevy sedan for only four hundred. The G.I. Bill will pay for my college tuition. With a part-time job I can have fun in the sun and learn something, too.

But, when the sun shines, how can I leave Seattle? All shades of green mixed with azaleas, rhododendrons, lilies, peonies, roses, black-eyed Susans, tall fir trees, deep blue sky, pure oxygenated air, and seventy-degree temperature. Can I leave my parents again and their extended family of loving church people?

I cough and spit out nicotine phlegm. Hush up, my brain throbs. It rains all the time here. I sit still in Mama's rocking chair and rethink what I just thought. I can't leave my good friend, Vera, a divorcée who works in the blueprint room. Yeah, I can. She has two little kids that her rich mom takes care of in Portland.

I stopped there once when they were all together. Her mom called me gauche because I refused a pair of her late husband's pajamas and slept in my underwear. Mama doesn't know about Vera.

Nor Joanne, the Catholic girl I sometimes go out with. Joanne's parents don't like Protestants.

I really like Betty and Rosemary from our church. Mama does, too. But Betty's father, Walter, doesn't like me. We went out for breakfast once. I put ketchup on my sunny-side-up eggs. Most everyone does that in the navy. Walter snickered, called me a hick, and used the word gauche, too.

Can I leave my playground basketball team or fast-pitch softball team? I'm the pitcher, and we're in first place in the "A" league. Man, I gotta have another cigarette and run to my car.

Elsie double parks her mother's car beside me. I stub out my cigarette and jump in the seat beside her.

She beams, "Mom says I can ride down to L.A. with you."

Whoa! Her mother is a straight-laced woman from a straight-laced church. Takes two days to get to L.A. Unless you want to switch drivers and speed nonstop on that narrow, winding Highway 99.

Elsie stops in her driveway. Her mom, Mary, rushes to the car. "Oh, Dale, I'm so glad you decided to go. I trust you with Elsie. I know you will have an enjoyable trip."

Mary, a former Alaska school teacher, holds my interest more than Elsie. I could talk to her all day. I think most mothers want to marry off their daughters by the time they're twenty years old. Wait a minute. Something's going on here.

Elsie drives to a soda fountain. The jukebox plays, "Cigarettes and whiskey, and wild, wild women. They'll drive you crazy, they'll drive you insane."

Elsie smiles, "I like chocolate."

I pinch off her straw sleeve. "How about Willie?" I think he's still her hot-headed Cajun boyfriend.

"Willie? I don't know."

"Crazy about you, I recall."

"Finishing up summer school, I think."

"Uh-huh," I grunt. "Pretty possessive?"

She frowns, "Mom doesn't like him."

"Uh-oh," this time I say under my breath. Takes only a second for the picture to develop in my mind. Mary wants me to take her daughter alone to California. She knows Willie will find out. Poof! There goes Willie.

I leer like Groucho Marx, "Long drive with me."

Elsie stares at me for a long time, then takes a cigarette from my package. I hold my Zippo lighter up, and she moves to the flame like a moth to a backyard barbecue. She inhales a little bit, coughs, and waves the smoke away from her face.

"This your first?"

"Yes, first time I inhaled."

For a whole week Mama walks around with a quizzical look after I tell her, "It's to save money. Share expenses."

I keep moving, too. I don't sit still long enough for her to quote the Bible or other proprieties to me.

We get on the road and run out of things to talk about after about two hours. Elsie takes over and drives to Eugene, Oregon, with me still awake. When I take over, she empties the ashtray on the parking lot. The word "gauche" comes to mind again. I hope I don't need those butts if I run out of cigarettes. She falls asleep with a hip pressed into mine.

That old Marine at my teenage filling station hangout pops up. He cautions, "Millions more babies would be born every year if men didn't exercise what little restraint they have." He says that while he watches the backsides of pretty women wiggle by.

Elsie's body pushes harder into mine. She stirs me. I can't drive anymore and pull into a rustic motel with a "Vacancy" sign. A light mist falls.

I shake Elsie half-awake. "Got any money?"

She hands me a twenty-dollar bill. Narrow rows of flat bricks line each side of a muddy walkway. I teeter back and forth on the bricks and run straight into the lobby with dry feet.

"How much for a room?"

The bored clerk looks up from her *True Romances* magazine. She spits out of the side of her mouth, "Six dollars."

"Give me two adjoining rooms."

Her eyes flicker. She looks out the door before she hands me the keys. She makes me feel weird. Why spend the extra six dollars?

I carry the bags and balance on the bricks while Elsie splashes down the middle of the muddy walkway. After I plop down her bag, I move to the door.

She gives me the same quizzical look I saw on the clerk's face.

She mumbles, "Wait, where are we?"

"Grant's Pass, Oregon. Good night."

She raps on the thin wall between us. "When do we get up?"

"Early," I holler and run water in the sink.

We reach Los Angeles late the next day. I park in back of the women's dorm, shake out the kinks, and open the trunk. I turn with Elsie's bag and bump into a guy. He hugs Elsie and asks her, "Drive nonstop from Seattle?"

"Nope. Willie, this is Dale," she replies. "Stopped in southern Oregon."

He persists, "Side of the road?"

"Nope. Motel."

She swivels her body away. Willie's face turns color. He slobbers into his red bandana handkerchief. I steel myself for his next question. In the same room?

He makes choking noises. No words come out. They stand nose to nose. I set her bag down, back out of the lot, and light up a cigarette before he clobbers me.

I've seen riled up Cajuns in the navy. They hold both hands together in a giant fist and slam down on someone's head. Pole-axed, they call it.

Four days later I sit near Elsie in the cafeteria. She waves her left hand at me. A large rock sparkles on her ring finger.

She giggles, "Me and Willie."

I give her a big epiphany smile of admiration. "Congratulations."

She outsmarted both her mother and me. Made Willie jealous enough to pop the question. I feel relieved. For once I don't need another cigarette. Any more may drive me crazy, may drive me insane.

MY SISTER'S SHADOW *by Dale Crum*

A slight squeak or scratch at Dad's back door flutters my eyelids. Prickles tickle my neck. I rise up from the sofa. Shake the cobwebs out. A burglar? The wind? A dream?

When did I fall asleep? When *Fibber McGee and Molly* went off the air, I guess.

In the dim light a ghostly shadow floats along a wall. Mama's grandfather clock strikes three. Rustles follow the shadow into the hall. Sounds that a woman's dress might make. A whiff of perfume tickles my nose.

Uh-huh, either my oldest sister, Cleo, or older sister, Marguerite. Gotta be Cleo. Marguerite, the valedictorian of her high-school senior class, doesn't go out much. She's going off to college on a full scholarship in a few days.

But Cleo, a twenty-year-old kindred spirit, underachieves like me. She came in late many times but never this late. And, to my knowledge, not sneaking in the back door. Who, what, kept her out so late?

I think about her latest boyfriend that I know about. A man in his twenties standing about six feet three nicknamed "Tinesy" for his height. Real name's Clarence, I think. I don't know whether he ever played basketball. My high-school team has only one boy over six feet tall.

Tinesy has some kind of county job but spends a lot of time in the local pool hall. An expert pool player who plays for money with about a dozen other pool sharks.

From time to time I watch him from across the room while he wins or loses quite a bit of money. The sheriff doesn't run me or my teenage friends out of the pool room as long as the proprietor says we are behaving.

Tinesy never looks me in the eye or acts like he wants to make friends with a sixteen-year-old. He strikes me as a man who's out for only one thing with my sister. Sex.

I decide to seek advice tomorrow from my good friend Milt. He has older sisters, too.

Morning comes. Cleo doesn't come to the breakfast table. Bright-eyed Marguerite sits across from me. My resentful eyes rove from Mama to Dad. I feel that my sisters get away with lots more than I.

What if I stayed out 'til three in the morning? These devout Christians would heap fire and brimstone on my head. Maybe they didn't hear Cleo come in last night. But they do know about her late dates.

Milt guffaws when I express my worry about my sister being with Tinesy.

"Dale, your nose hangs out of joint a mile. None of your business what your sister does. You don't trust Cleo, and your parents do? How funny."

"But Milt, my parents seem out of touch. You and I raise hell all over this town. They never hear about it. They don't know about Tinesy. My sister needs protection."

"From fast guys like Tinesy? Buy her a box of condoms. What protection do other guys' sisters have from you?"

I blink, "That's different. Can I stand by and watch my own sister...?"

"Become a fast woman?" He hoots, "Excuse me, did I say that? She might become an old maid. They call every single girl an old maid if she's over twenty-one."

I shrug, "So what?"

"Girls have to circulate. Find somebody. Parents know that. Geez, you stupid ass."

"Um, Milt, how much do you know about Tinesy?"

"Like most single men in this town, drinks beer, shoots pool, fortunate to have a job, chases girls. What would you hope to hear? That he goes to church two or three times a week? Let me tell you about some churchgoing, whore-hopping guys I know."

"Cleo doesn't go with church guys. Claims they're too sissified."

He sneers, "Sounds like what my sisters might say about you, Dale. Have you had your ashes hauled lately?"

"I don't kiss and tell, Milt. I don't feel sissified. Better watch out for your sisters."

"Oh, ho, Casanova. You don't worry me."

He cackles like the Shadow. Only the Shadow knows what evil lies in the hearts of men.

Hmmm, Marguerite will leave for college soon. Cleo may find a husband. I will become the oldest in the family, with my younger sister and two brothers looking up to me.

I won't have to share a birthday cake with Cleo, who has her birthday two days before mine. Also, if I find some fast girl, I won't have two tattle-tale sisters to rat me out. I will inherit a better room in the house, too.

In the evening everyone except Cleo gathers around the radio for the *Jack Benny* program. Near the end a tall shadow silhouettes itself on the screen door. Cleo and Tinesy come in holding hands. Gee! First time, I believe, that he has set foot inside our house. He seems taller than he does at the pool hall. Looks me in the eye for the first time.

Cleo wraps her arms around him and gushes, "Daddy, Mama, we have something—"

Dad waves his arms. "Shhh, later, later. I want to hear Dennis and Rochester."

I make room on the sofa. Only after the last Jell-O commercial and the orchestra plays "Hooray for Hollywood" does Dad turn off the radio and swivel back to Cleo.

Tinesy clears his throat. He and Cleo blurt out, "We got married last night."

Dead silence compresses our living room. Time and space seem to disappear, as predicted by Einstein.

Mama dabs her eyes. "Cleo and Clarence. What a nice sound! That's wonderful. Congratulations!"

She jumps up and gives them both a big hug. She may never use his nickname, "Tinesy."

Dad extends his hand to Clarence. "You got a mighty fine woman for a wife. Where do you plan to live?"

"With my folks for awhile. Had to work today. Tonight we're going twenty miles away to Mammoth Spring for a couple days."

He bends down and whispers in my ear. "I'll teach you how to stroke, not hit, a cue ball someday soon. Put some English on it."

I steal a glance at Cleo's radiant face. Oh, no, she may cause Clarence to hang up his cue stick for good.

———•••———

Karl Grey   *Karl grew up in Texas, the son of a band leader of the 1920s and 1930s (and later a booking agent for Jelly Roll Morton and others) and the singer in his father's band. Karl's father barely knew his son and died when Karl was very young. His mother later married but maintained dreams of celebrity, style, and status. Karl was a hindrance to her, and she never let him forget it.*

THE GARAGE   *by Karl Grey*

If I hold my breath just like I do when I shoot and brace my arm against my leg just right, I can paint the chrome strip on my model car so good that nobody will be able to tell it's painted by hand. I love building model cars. I love painting all the detail on them that I can, because nobody else I know can do it as good as I can, and that's what has won me trophies for the last two summers at Mrs. Sherman's Lakewood Hobby Shop.

The sweat on my leg—with my arm braced against it—is starting to make me slip, but if I can hold on long enough I can finish this strip down the side panel of my '55 Chevy convertible. Man, is it ever hot. It'd sure be a lot better if she held these contests in the wintertime, then I wouldn't have to sweat so much when I'm painting. I guess I could wait until it's a cooler time, but right now all I want to do is paint my '55. Besides, a summer night in Texas is about as cool as it's going to be for a while anyway.

In the background I can hear the sound of the air conditioner in the window in the den and the TV turned up too loud so that my mother and stepfather can hear it while they are washing the supper dishes. The door from the den to the kitchen is shut so the den will stay cool, but they want to hear *The Ed Sullivan Show* until the dishes are done. My mother washes, and my stepdad dries, and they have their drinks, scotch and water over ice, until they're done. My stepdad tells her all about what went on during the day at work, and she says, "Uh-huh."

I have all my windows open, but I keep the curtains shut so that nobody can see me in my room at night. The only way I can stay cool enough is to sit in my underwear. I wouldn't mind if somebody saw me in my underwear if I wasn't so fat. In fact, if I wasn't so fat, I would probably walk around in my underwear in front of people. If I wasn't so fat, the sweat would roll straight down my body and make me look better, like the guys in *Strength and Health* magazine. My sweat just gets caught in the creases between the rolls of my fat, and then it mixes with whatever dirt is on my body to make "fat mud," which isn't too bad until I stand up. When I stand up, I look like I have stripes on my body. My belly button really gets the worst of it, but nobody can see that. I just have to make sure I dig it out when I shower, otherwise it smells bad.

The model contest is a week away, and because I'm such a good painter I think I can win a first-place trophy this time. The other kids use model putty to make some pretty neat-looking custom cars, but none of them can paint as good as I can. Crap! The paint's running. What caused that? Now I have to take all the paint off and start over, and that can make the plastic look bad if I don't get it off right. There it is, a little piece of molding overrun on the chrome strip. Why didn't I see that when I was shaving it with my X-ACTO blade? Too late now, all I can do is take it off and start over.

I can hear the sound of the locusts outside, the whir of the air conditioner in the den, and the faint sound of conversation in the kitchen. I have to go to the garage to get my trimming blades. I wish I hadn't left them there, but Billy Pike wanted me to carve notches into his six-shooter, and my mother won't allow him into the house.

"Billy Pike is not the right kind of person to be in my house. He'll mess things up, and then you won't clean it up. You never do."

So I had to take my blade kit outside. At least I'll get to cool off when I go through the den. As I stand up, the sweat in the folds of my fat rolls down my body and catches in the waistband of my underwear. As I open the door to the den, the blast of cool air hits my wet skin. Ahh, that's more like it.

"And now, tonight, on this stage—"

I pause to see who is going to be on *Ed Sullivan* and to get as cool as I can. Buddy Hackett. I keep walking, through the other door from the den to the kitchen. There they are, my mother and my stepfather. Their backs to me, facing the window over the sink. She is washing with her drink off to her left, and he is drying with his drink off to his right. I bet they don't even hear me. My mother removes her hand from the suds, picks up her drink with the sudsy Playtex Living glove.

They hear me. She says, "Close the door! Do you think we're trying to air condition the whole house? Where do you think you're going like that?"

"I'm just going to get something in the garage," and I open the door. Shit! The outside garage door to the street is open, and I already shut the kitchen door. I don't want to go all the way back to my room to get something else on . . . I'll just turn off the light. I know just where the X-ACTO kit is. I can just run out and grab it and run back in and nobody will see me.

I hit the light switch, run into the dark, and grab the X-ACTO kit. Slam! Click! All of a sudden, the lights are on, and I am exposed to the neighborhood, standing in the garage in my underwear.

Panic seizes me. I feel ashamed and embarrassed. Through the door I can hear my mother laughing. I drop the kit and start to pound on the door. I'm pulling at the handle and hitting the door.

"Please let me in! Please unlock the door." I can hear my mother on the other side laughing at me. I'm pounding on the door, and I'm sure the whole neighborhood can see me in my underwear. They have all come out of their houses and are standing in the dark street watching me like I'm on the screen at a drive-in movie. I can hear them laughing at me and my mother laughing at me and I can't stand the way I feel. I am so filled with panic.

I pound and pound on the door, but all I hear is the echo of laughing from both sides colliding on me. It's like this dream that I have over and over. I am walking on a sidewalk when all of a sudden I'm naked. I want to hide so that the other people on the sidewalk don't see me, so I duck around behind the row of trees that is between the street and the sidewalk, but the street is full of cars and all of the drivers can see me, so I go back around the trees, but then the sidewalk people can see me and pretty soon they have all stopped and all of the cars have stopped and they are all laughing and blowing the horns and saying, "Look at the naked fat kid. Does he even have a dick?" The sound gets louder and louder and I can't get away.

CRASH!

The kitchen door flies off the hinges and wood splinters as it hits the stove on the other side of the kitchen. I am in the house before the door hits the ground. My mother screams, and the scotch and water breaks on the floor. My stepfather has his belt undone by now and is pulling it through the loops of his pants.

I am running, into the den, into the cool . . . and my back stings, again and again, as I drop to the floor and roll myself into a ball and take it on my back. I'm safe now. I'm inside myself, and nobody can see me while he continues to hit me with the doubled-up belt.

"Thank you ladies and gentlemen, it's been a really big shoooow tonight. Next week on this stage, Elvis Presley" . . . and the crowd screams and my back stings, but it's cool in here and nobody can see me.

———— • • • ————

CJ Schepers   *CJ Schepers is a professional ghostwriter and book editor living in Los Angeles. A former news journalist and ad copywriter, she has been writing since age twelve. After surviving a childhood that nearly crushed her, CJ found creative writing to be profoundly freeing and healing. This chapter is from her novel-in-progress* Blackcat-Whitecat: The Interdimensional Tails, *about two immortal cat beings that exist on a plane of existence far beyond what most humans know. They are on a mission to retrieve a human soul, stolen and frozen in time by a demon angel. As the story builds, the interdimensional cats move in and out of Earth's timeline, and are pulled deeper and deeper into the complex, intertwining lives of humans.*

BLACKCAT-WHITECAT   *by C J Schepers*

Chapter 2

Bent on one knee, she is perched atop a small ice-frosted ridge, in another dimension hidden far from the world she'd once known. A cloak falls across her like liquid silver, and solid wisps of golden hair frame her narrow face. Godforsaken mountain peaks, cragged and sharpened with more age than any creature can imagine, stretch out in infinite agony beneath a starless canopy of thick gray sky.

A Scepter of Wonder as tall as the Sword of All Time balances itself between her cold childlike hands. But the most unusual part are the wings—solid as stone and three times the length of her body. Jutting out from her marblesque shoulders, their innermost curves arc toward her like the crescent Moon of Earth. Her irises, as vivid as sapphires, are locked behind pale, colorless eyelids. If only she could open them. But she is frozen in time. Or, at least, her Astral Soul is, in a place where not even the wind knows how to howl..."

Arcelia's fair fur shivered as she privately recounted the great Purisima's telling of the abduction and merciless captivity of the human female named Ruby. It was something she and Magico had secretly shared ever since the great ones, Purisima and Sirius, had enlightened them as to their purpose back on Earth. It had been the crime of eternity, one that was quickening with every second, reaching out in infinite tendrils of darkness and destruction. Even for evolved catkins as themselves, it seemed a preposterous, doomed mission. Arcelia imagined what it would be like to lose her own Astral Soul, to be permanently severed like that. Her heart began to quake as though she were fending off some mortally vicious attack.

Sunrise was coming. Even though her eyes were closed, Arcelia could sense it shifting between the edges of the dark and the light. Her lithe form sat upright in the Lotus position, and the breathing was purposeful, measured. It was a vain attempt to push away the story of Ruby, and the thoughts of what had led to the seizing of the human's soul. As far as anyone knew it was something that had *never* happened in all the levels of all the worlds and infinite time. But such thoughts only clamored about in Arcelia's consciousness, and the more she pushed them away, the more they demanded to be heard.

"Our concern, of course, is the rip in the spectrum of our interconnected cosmos and the shared Divine Will of all living kind," Sirius had told them with the gravest of voice. Arcelia reflected on the memory of the great blackcat's saffron eyes pulsating fiercely in the twilight of their astral garden amid the Gingkos. She sucked in the deepest breath and held it for a long, long moment. Nonetheless, the words of the great ones continued haunting her. "We can no more be neutral in this matter." Purisima's chest had risen and fell like crashing waves, the gold that encircled her throat with the eye of The Whole One heaving with it. "It is already beginning to affect the galaxy's chaotic order."

At this point, Arcelia realized that she might as well allow the story in her mind to re-tell itself as it had since they first learned of it, dozens of times. Perhaps there was a clue, a sign, a solution that they had all failed to see.

"I want to be an angel," Ruby, the human, had thinly whispered into the air one grey winter night. And, someone had heard her. It had been the first misstep across the ripples of all the universes. It had the potential to unravel into the ultimate tragedy for life kind, *all* of it. It had nothing to do with Ruby declaring that she wished for such a thing. It had everything to do with the one who had heard it. It had been *him*, Lahash, one of many fallen angels, true enough. "But this one," Arcelia recalled the words of Purisima, as she finished telling she and Magico what they needed to know. "This one, Lahash, he has a particular panache for stealing one's prayers and silent hopes, not to mention stirring awake the darkest spots in the darkest of hearts...." Arcelia couldn't help but notice that Purisima's front claws had instantly protracted at that moment, gleaming in the inky night air like freshly polished daggers. Even the great one seemed oblivious she had done so.

"...He is the one who has dared interfere with *all* our Divine Wills." Arcelia finished this last thought out loud to herself, for Magico was already away on a hunt with the first Earth cat that had crossed their paths since arriving to Earth only moments ago.

Yes, Lahash had once been a great angel; in fact, Guardian Master over thousands of other angel beings. Unfortunately, the centuries of power and authority had made him only ravenous for more. No one had seen his face in more than three thousand years, not since The One Goodness of all the galaxies had him expelled for his unforgivable crime: assembling an army of angels to steal the prayers of a human. The details of those prayers never did reach The One Goodness. They were lost forever, in turn, throwing the course of all life significantly off-kilter from that of Divine Will's.

It could have been worse, far worse for *everyone*. Despite the fact that no living creature or spirit had spoke firsthand of what this demon angel looked like, word of his presence managed to replicate itself. Generations upon generations of catkins had passed down the specifics, millennium after millennium: Lahash and his smooth, elegant words. Lahash and his dark, handsome hair that draped across the milk-white shoulders of his naked torso; the cloven feet that dangled beneath his long, black skirt. Lahash and those wings—such magnificent wings of layered feathers that soared above his chiseled head like a proud, ferocious bird. Then there was the symbol of Inca seared into his massive chest and the two slender glistening swords that he carried across his back.

"Beware," Sirius had warned them. "His weapons are not of the physical world." The tail of the great blackcat bristled forth like a thousand quills and his red-blue-gold wings began to billow wildly. "But make no mistake," Sirius's voice boomed louder, as the flapping of his wings grew fiercer, and hundreds upon thousands of Gingko leaves fell from their mother tree's delicate limbs, "they can slice through any steel, flesh, or bone as easily as a swift seizer's talons through cream." And, just as quickly as it had begun, those massive wings of his stilled themselves.

It was the last hard wind, Arcelia thought, *the eerie stillness just before a terrible storm.* The four age-versed catkins stood silently staring at the mounds of leaves that had buried their feet. Arcelia's snowy coat shivered, and she closed her eyes trying to remember everything she knew. . . .

On that particular Earth night in that particular sliver of time and space, Lahash had stumbled upon Ruby's request for barely a moment before speaking to her in her dreams. His words, Lahash's words, had found their way in and stuck to her like barnacles on a ship, "When you hear 6 . . . 8 . . . 9, my dearest Ruby, you shall have it."

The moment that Ruby realized someone had heard and meant to grant her this wish, no more than a strong thought, she immediately spoke up to cancel the request. "Wait! I don't think I really want that, I just realized. I would like it not to happen for a very, very long time, not until I'm old and wrinkled and gray, and Eddy is gone and my children are in love and well cared for, please, but thank you. I prefer to wait a long, long—yes, a very long time."

Ruby woke from that dream to a family of sparrows chirping in the orange bougainvilleas that crawled their way up the wall of the neighbor's garage. The squirrel was clacking its mouth off as it scurried across the hot brown roof. She fumbled for her glasses on the nightstand, the memory of Lahash's face melting as fast as ice in warm-blooded hands.

It was Saturday, and Ruby and Eddy had decided to spend it lazily in the strangest of places: a giant shopping mall, filled with the buzz of ordinary humans doing ordinary things to pass the time of their ordinary lives. Ruby was taking her sweet time trying on gloves at a small vintage boutique. Even for a patient man like Eddy it was taking longer than he cared for. He told Ruby that he'd wait outside for her but by the time she'd finished, he was gone. She kept checking her phone. No one seemed to notice her mounting panic as she nervously pushed her way through the crowd. An old, familiar sense of abandonment slithered its way ever so quickly, enveloping her like a hungry python. She closed her eyes and tried to say a prayer, but it seemed so trite and pointless. Instead she began weaving more frantically through the mob of shoppers, on the hunt for Eddy. The glimpse of something red caught her heart: there he was, his dingy red baseball cap bopping in and out of the sea of life. She released all of her breath, which had been stuck in her throat like a child's toy in a narrow drainpipe, and sprinted off. She was a quarterback near the end zone with only ten seconds left on the clock when she finally reached him, leaping so hard into his arms, that she nearly knocked them both to the ground.

Eddy's eyes glistened like chocolate jewels and she purred into his good ear, the right one. "Let's go home," Eddy said, his mouth breaking into mischief. He squeezed her hand off and on, as they made their way outside. Out of nowhere a gust caught the brim of Ruby's pink hat, the one Eddy had bought her on the boardwalk their very first summer together. His arm thrust out to catch it like a viper striking, and they both laughed in surprise. "Whew, that was a close one!" she laughed.

Across the street a tall Italian looking man with dark curly hair was dragging the arm of a little girl, who couldn't be more than four years old. "Look at that," Ruby said, turning to Eddy. A circular saw started spinning in her gut. The traffic light had changed and shoppers were crossing the street, but the little girl wasn't moving. Without warning, her father swung his right foot wrapped in a brown leather boot, and kicked her from behind. "Whadda I say?!" The girl tipped violently forward, and as a toy weighted at the bottom, she bounced right back.

Ruby's hand dropped Eddy's. Her vision narrowed as she charged toward the man who was half a mountain taller than most. He was yanking his daughter in the opposite direction now, away from the crowd, and a sick chill pop-fired across the membranes of Ruby's mind. She didn't even see the silver car coming at forty miles per hour. Normally, she was as cautious as a girl scout when it came to crossing city streets. Her body flew up and did a shocking vertical somersault, landing with a sickening crunch on the hood as the driver hammered the brakes. Somewhere in the million conversations happening at once; through the *bong-bong clump, bong-bong clump* of the drummer down the street; the pigeons cooing; and the homeless man dressed in all black rags and shaking his cup of coins, Ruby heard Eddy scream. Next thing she knew he was clutching her in his arms, and the siren one hears without much regard drew closer.

Eddy was trembling. "Don't let me die," Ruby begged him. In the loud, frenetic chorus of the living, she heard something else in the distant...6...8...9. Suddenly, to her horror, Eddy's mouth began to shrink. "Eddy..." Her voice seemed so strange to her, raspy and faint and faraway. "Don't worry, baby. I–I–can fix this." Eddy's mouth was nothing but a pinhole now, and his face fading fast, except for those warm-brown eyes.

Ruby felt herself being yanked from her body by an invisible hand. It was the opposite of gravity. Instead of falling to Earth she was rising. There was a force of something outside, yet inside her, too. It was the strangest feeling in the world. Sounds of heavy wet sheets flapping in the wind forced her to turn her head apprehensively over her shoulder. And there, she saw it: wings jutting out of her back. Wings!

Suddenly Ruby felt strong as a god, and realized she was floating. Below her, Ruby saw Eddy holding onto her broken body. Her body's eyes were open but without light. Ambulance workers and firemen were trying to pry him away from her. Ruby continued soaring higher and higher and higher, taking in the surreal scene of her own life and death. Was this a dream? She remembered the nightmare from this morning, and a primal scream rang out of her mouth. But it was too late. From somewhere behind the fast-approaching clouds she heard a deep voice singing, and it wasn't Ol' Blue Eyes.

"I've gotttt youuuu...under my skinnn..."

Afterword:
The Life-Story Writing Workbooks

In today's fast-paced world, quality jobs and careers require that workers be able to think clearly. They need to understand and communicate points of view other than their own and to do so using language that is both persuasive and to the point.

In this type of environment, many adult learners of English—whether they are learning English as a second language, or perhaps struggled with or were poorly taught English when they were younger—get left behind.

An effective literacy program to help these learners develop writing skills must provide simple methods of teaching and learning. At the same time, the program must arouse the students' interest in writing while opening their minds to the possibilities of mastering writing in the English language.

What kind of writing method best motivates students to *want* to write while also teaching them writing skills? Well, most people love to tell stories about their own experiences. Thus an effective writing program must also involve storytelling. With this in mind, I created the "writing from within" writing program.

Everyone, even very young students (5th and 6th graders), can learn to write well using the building blocks of storytelling—narrative, dialogue, and the expression of inner thoughts and feelings—upon which this method is based.

What about analytical skills, essay writing, and the like? Aren't these aspects of writing important? Indeed they are. Strong essay writing requires that writers engage the reader even as they demonstrate the essay and research writing skills (using persuasive devices such as comparing and contrasting, reasons, classification, definition, etc.) required of all incoming college students. However, the mistake we educators have made in the past is asking students to undertake complex writing tasks way too early in their process of developing writing skills.

Common sense suggests that we simplify the process: First teach students to engage the reader (and themselves) in their writing, and then pay attention to the acquisition of analytical skills.

What are these "engagement" skills that students needs to learn? Again, they are the same skills employed in storytelling: narrative, dialogue, and the expression of inner thoughts and feelings. If we as teachers can show students how to translate their love of storytelling onto the written page, then we are well on our way to providing them with the skills and motivation they need to write effectively and successfully.

Beyond that, storytelling skills can lead students in two important directions: awareness of the "self" in their own stories (character) and awareness of relationships between other people.

When a student writes a story about himself or herself, the story becomes a reflection of the writer's character qualities. We teachers can guide students to an understanding of how the story mirrors their own character qualities and, through that, help them understand themselves.

In thirty years of working with students from all walks of life, especially those from less-than-privileged circumstances, I have seen that all too often they find themselves at the mercy of a world they didn't make long before they understand what relationships are about. As educators, our obligation to our students is to begin to teach them the process of understanding (and writing about) relationships early in their education.

This matrix of writing skills and life-understanding will provide the student with a basis for thinking (in time, objectively and analytically) about the world of ideas, the world of opposing points of view, and the search for "truth" in art, in literature, and in life.

All of these skills are taught in the "writing from within" method of writing life stories as laid out in the book *Writing from Within* (1988, 1990, 1998, 2004, 2013), my manual for teachers *In Your Own Voice* (1993, 2004), and a series of workbooks entitled Life-Story Writing Workbooks (2010).

Life-Story Writing Workbook I: Storytelling teaches students basic storytelling skills. It enables them to make clear their points of view about life experiences as well as express how they feel as the experience takes place.

Life-Story Writing Workbook II: The Storyteller's Path to Essay and Research Writing demonstrates how acquiring storytelling skills can help to create a viable transition to analytical and thoughtful academic writing.

Life-Story Writing Workbook III: Self-Assessment/Relationship helps students understand themselves by looking at their own character qualities as reflected in the story they have just written. As students become familiar with character qualities, they have an opportunity to look at the two principal factors that make up relationships of all kinds: power and love.

Taken together, these workbooks will:

1. engender in students a love of writing and self-expression
2. create an understanding of what makes a story effective
3. enable students to apply the principles of storytelling to writing analytical essays
4. usher students into the world of the "examined" life
5. help students grasp the competing forces that make relationships either successful or difficult

Comments from those who have used the "writing from within" method, the Life-Story Writing Workbooks, and my teacher-training workshops appear at the start of this book. For further information about any of these, or to order copies of the Life-Story Writing Workbooks, please contact me at BernardSelling.com.

Other Books by Bernard Selling

Character Consciousness: From Self-Awareness to Creativity. This book moves the experience of personal writing from the technical arena of "how to write well" into "how can we see ourselves in our writing" in a way that not only produces self-awareness but opens the door to greater creativity.

The Art of Seeing: Appreciating Motion Pictures as an Art Form and as a Business. Hollywood has created a mass audience that appreciates film in a certain way—appealing to emotions. But contemporary audiences wonder whether there might be other, more interesting ways to appreciate films. This book outlines that other way of experiencing films—by *seeing* into what's on screen in the same way that painters of the past nurtured their viewers' ability to "see" what was around them.

Please go to BernardSelling.com for more information about these books.

———— •••• ————

The Writing from Within Series:

Writing from Within: The Next Generation. A semi-bestseller, with over 65,000 copies sold, *Writing from Within* has provided an abundance of techniques and solutions to the problems of writing life stories. Leapfrog Press called it "A seminal work in the field of autobiographical writing." This 25th Anniversary Edition integrates the best material from *Writing from Within* and the more-advanced material from *Writing from Deeper Within* into a fully rewritten book, the latest and best edition of *Writing from Within.*

Writing from Deeper Within goes deeper into the writing process, examining the components of great storytelling and expanding on the "writing from within" method. Selling describes how writers can reach and resolve a story's climax, get to the heart of their characters, and incorporate backstory and history using advanced writing strategies. He also discusses how life stories can be turned into creative stories, novels, and even screenplays.

The *Writing from Within Workbook* contains step-by-step exercises for successful life-story writing. Includes lessons on how to start, how to access and write early memories, and how to revise. Later units explain how to add narrative, inner thoughts and dialogue, character sketches, and climaxes. Sample rewrites show how your stories can grow and develop into longer forms. Available in paperback and spiral-bound editions.

For more information and to order these books visit hunterhouse.com.

NOTES

Printed in the USA
CPSIA information can be obtained
at www.ICGtesting.com
JSHW062127290124
56258JS00016B/607

9 780897 936309